Dedication

To the Benedictine Sisters of Covington, Kentucky,
in whose School of the Lord's Service
I first learned about the human side of the psalms.

Making the
PSALMS
your
PRAYER

INSIGHTS • EXERCISES • RESOURCES

RENEE
RUST

Nihil Obstat: Rev. Thomas Richstatter, O.F.M.
                  Rev. John J. Jennings

Imprimi Potest: Rev. Jeremy Harrington, O.F.M.
                    Provincial

Imprimatur: + James H. Garland, V.G.
                Archdiocese of Cincinnati
                October 1, 1987

Unless otherwise indicated, quotations from the Psalms in this book are from *Psalms Anew* by Maureen Leach and Nancy Schreck, ©1986, Saint Mary's Press, Winona, MN, 55987, and are used by permission.

Scripture texts in this book marked "NAB" are taken from the *New American Bible,* copyright ©1970 by the Confraternity of Christian Doctrine, Washington, D.C., and are used by permission of the copyright owner. All rights reserved.

"Psalm 23" (modern Jewish version) is from *Blues of the Sky: A Poet's Bible,* published by Ultramarine Publishing Co., Hastings-on-Hudson, NY, 10706, and is used by permission of David Rosenberg, ©1976, 1987.

"Psalm 23" (Cherokee Indian version) is from *The Bible Reader: An Interfaith Interpretation,* Bruce Publishing Co., New York, 1969.

"Ode 19" and non-biblical "Psalm 11" are from *The Other Bible,* Willis Barnstone, ed., copyright ©1984 by Willis Barnstone. Reprinted by permission of Bantam Books, Inc. All rights reserved.

Psalm compositions by the author were previously published by the College Press, Kettering, OH, 45429, and are copyrighted as follows: "My Childhood Speaks to Christ" ©1983; "Psalm of Disgust," "Let Me Pray On," "Psalm in Praise of Life's Journey" (adapted for this publication), "Psalm of a Worrier," "God of the Hopeful," "A Psalmic Ballad for David: Shepherd, Sinner, King," ©1985; "Psalm at Virginia Beach" (adapted for this publication) ©1986.

Cover design by David Diehl

Book design by Julie Lonneman

ISBN 0-86716-082-9

Contents

Introduction

The psalms *are* prayers. They came to the lips of Israel's people as easily as the Lord's Prayer comes to ours. These ancient songs have nourished the faith of the great Hebrew prophets and the great saints of the Christian era. Jesus learned them at Mary's knee. And they still have the power to enrich the prayer life of modern believers.

The purpose of this book is to lead the reader into the heart of the psalms and to uncover there the world of feelings, imagination and ordinary concerns which give the psalms such a timeless quality. Practical exercises encourage recasting modern everyday experience in the psalmist's language.

Chapter One offers an overview of the psalms—their origins, their poetic nature and the images of God they employ—as well as an introduction to the Hebrew spirituality in which they are grounded. This exploration of our Judeo-Christian heritage uncovers the connections between the psalmist and the modern pray-er.

Chapter Two looks at some of the problems 20th-century believers have with the psalms: their sometimes harsh language and their violent imagery. Considering healthy reactions to real evil leads to practical ways of bringing the "cursing psalms" into harmony with gospel spirituality.

Chapter Three faces the confusion in the psalter and explains the inherent differences between oral and written prayers, between private and communal prayer. It offers exercises in "dwelling on a psalm" as one means of dealing with the disorder.

The next three chapters present a threefold division of the psalms: hymns of praise, lamentations, prayers of trust. Each type reflects a basic human mood; each contains specific elements and employs certain images of God. The reader is encouraged to become a psalmist and write a personal version of each.

Chapter Seven explores how universal human themes—sex, politics and religion—are prayerfully addressed in the psalms and also in other biblical and extra-biblical writings.

Appendix A offers more exercises in psalm-prayer; Appendix B presents an overview of available translations, musical resources and models for communal prayer.

A Note About Numbers

There are two numbering systems used for the Psalms: the original Hebrew and the Greek-Latin. Because of a difference in the way the psalms are divided, the Hebrew numbering varies from the Greek-Latin by one digit through most of the psalter. The familiar Good Shepherd Psalm, for example, is Psalm 22 in the Greek-Latin version, Psalm 23 in the Hebrew system. Most recent editions of the Bible (including the New Jerusalem, New American, New English and Good News Bibles) use the Hebrew—as does this book.

1. What Are the Psalms?

An Overview

"I never really used the psalms for praying," says a 79-year-old woman. "They've always been a puzzle to me."

A man in his mid-50's, an active participant in a parish Bible study group, speaks with surprise. "We did a lot of Scripture study on the Gospels, but I didn't know the psalms—the *Book* of Psalms, is that right?—could help me pray so much!"

A 22-year-old graduate student who has worked through a major rejection in her life reports that psalmody gave her words to pray through the wrenching loss, anger, confusion.

The psalms are centuries-old prayer grounded in Hebrew spirituality. The Book of Psalms found in the Old Testament (the Hebrew Scriptures) is a collection of 150 biblical psalms. The psalms emerge from a people who are in love with life and want to see good—or better—days (see Psalm 34:12). Each generation passes these time-tested prayers on to the next. Passed on but never passed over—such is the prayer book called Psalms.

The God of the psalmists is the God of Israel, the God of the Covenant. And this God is interested in human troubles, triumphs and trust. This God initiated the relationship with Israel in the first place by calling Abraham and Sarah to leave their old neighborhood and move on to a new place. The same God invited Moses to come right up to the burning bush and learn the divine name. The psalms celebrate this relationship with God.

Psalms Express Hebrew Spirituality

The classic stories of Abraham and Moses dramatize the kind of God to whom they, their followers and, eventually, Jesus related.

When Yahweh invited Abraham to leave his country, his family and his father's house (see Genesis 12:1), Abraham faced a choice about a different life-style with a lot of unknowns. Was he open to God's voice because he was searching for new meaning and direction in his life, because the old gods and values of Chaldea were dead to him?

In any case, a living God asked Abraham for faith and trust and a willingness to cut his cultural umbilical cords. It was a personal invitation to new opportunities. To move on would require Abraham's determination and hope. His experience of a God who addressed him by name and promised to travel with him made Abraham ready.

I imagine Sarah was glad to hear that a divine Someone was talking about being on their side for a change: "I will bless those who bless you;/and curse those who curse you," the Someone had said (Genesis 12:3a, NAB). It looked like better times were ahead.

Their geographical journey was only part of a larger leap Abraham and Sarah were being called to take. In centuries to come the people of the covenant, the Jews, would recall and celebrate the breakthrough God made with this brave couple. Their biological parenthood would give way to something new again: the surprising role of mothering and fathering multitudes in their faith.

Psalmists would later lovingly incorporate into their prayer God's invitation to Abraham and Sarah: "Forget your people and your ancestor's home" (Psalm 45:10). The marvel of a God who wanted to come closer to humanity was cause for singing: "God remembers the covenant forever: the promise for a thousand generations,/the pact made with Abraham and Sarah..." (Psalm 105:8-9a).

The story of Moses demonstrates how the God celebrated in Hebrew spirituality pursues human beings. Here was a young man who had killed an Egyptian, a member of the class ruling over the Hebrews. A fugitive fleeing from a murder charge, Moses was making a life on his own in Midian when he became aware that some fearsome voice was calling him by name. Was someone finally catching up with him? A startled Moses had no time to determine who was speaking before he found himself responding, as if in a dream, to the words of the beckoner.

No sooner did he try to move closer to the Presence he was feeling than he was told not to do so. Was he imagining things? Too much desert sun perhaps? Moses had to stop and take off his shoes in the customary manner of a worshiper entering the temple.

Fascinated and fearful all at the same time, Moses persevered. His encounter with the One who spoke eerie words to his inner self—"I am who am" (Exodus 3:14a, NAB)—left him strangely assured. Evidently the speaker wanted to leave some mystery between them but also wanted to lead Moses beyond solitary confinement. In his aloneness Moses needed another presence; he now felt invited to go on to the greater things which that Presence was proposing.

After much struggle with the risks entailed, Moses decided to take on a leadership role in the midst of the very people he had left behind. He had the personal promise of the Mysterious One in the burning bush that he would have help. Something convinced him that Yahweh, the I AM, meant every word.

Later the people Moses led would give thanks and praise for a God who wanted to be with those who, like Moses, are down and out. Moses' experience revealed Yahweh's care and commitment early on. This story became part of Hebrew psalmody as it consistently celebrates a God with whom people can get involved, a God who wants to be among us to create possibilities.

Moses' experience led to the Exodus event, when the Chosen People escaped their oppressive conditions because of the partnership established between God and Moses. Psalm 114 is jubilant about the escape from Egypt which changed their history for all time.

The God of Hebrew spirituality gives clear signals about wanting to be known personally, to be active in human lives and to do what is necessary to make a difference in the world.

5

In the psalms we find examples of Yahweh giving guidance to those invited to such a relationship. Psalm 89 attests to God's faithful involvement; many other psalms portray God as the one who answers those in distress (91:15) and advises those who ask (25:8-9).

This God is different from the divinity portrayed in other religious traditions. Some Eastern prayer honors divinity in the form of a cosmic unity or world harmony. One Native American prayer expresses the worshiper's reverent pursuit of the Great Spirit throughout the land but gives little if any indication that this Divine Presence moves toward the human person or the human situation. These differences do not argue for one tradition's superiority over another, but underline the distinct kind of God who appears in the psalms. Yahweh is personally concerned about the welfare of humanity; the God present to our hearts and minds can be approached immediately and in very personal terms.

The psalmist relates primarily to Yahweh as the God of opportunity rather than a nature god. Yahweh wants to bring a future out of our desperate situations and order out of chaos. In other words, in times of sickness God is interested in healing; in the face of injustice the Just One wants righteousness; during loneliness Emmanuel, God-with-us, simply wants to be present. The psalmist knows this willingness from experience (111:26-31).

In the psalms people pray in a very personalized fashion. All human emotions (sorrow, hope, joy, hate, revenge, reward, planning, warring, and dealing with love and death) are characters in the great drama of life as perceived by the Hebrew sensibility. (Chapter Two will deal with some of the uncomfortable emotions certain Christians resist in the psalms.)

Psalms Are Songs to Be Sung

Psalmody is the *music* of the Jewish people at prayer. They sing together about their conflicts, health, day-to-day survival, relationships, national dignity and other concerns of mutual interest. I like to call these 150 psalms the "top 150" songs. For thousands of years this people sang out about what was nearest and dearest to their hearts. Off key or on, accompanied by a lyre or zither, they sang.

We are at a disadvantage if our first contact with the psalms is in written form. Texts contained so neatly on a printed page can deceive us with their calm appearance. We miss the vibrant tones of poetic songs delivered live from the lips of people who are willing to trust not only God but also one another with their heartfelt pain and praise.

Some psalms seem to arise from private petitions: for example, pleading for a cure to a serious illness. We can all identify with making such a prayer for ourselves or for someone we love; but most of the time *we* end up praying alone. The psalmist, on the other hand, extends personal prayer into the awareness of others and gets them to join in aloud on what might otherwise be a private plea. Psalmists know we need all the help we can get, and their gift is to enlarge private prayer so others can join in.

The psalmist often expressed the community's prayer around a public matter or a shared experience of God. At the enthronement of a king, for example, the psalmist led the people in public prayer for the ruler, typically asking Yahweh's blessing on the reign to make it just and peaceful. Today we can still pray most of Psalm 72 when presidents, religious leaders, local officials—even committee chairs—begin a term of service. Try thinking of a newly elected or appointed leader as you prayerfully read this psalm:

> O God, with your judgment and with your justice,
> endow the leaders.
> They shall govern your people with justice
> and your afflicted ones with righteousness.
> The mountains will bring peace for the people,
> and the hills justice.
> They shall defend the afflicted among the people,
> save the children of the poor,
> and crush the oppressor.
> May they endure as long as the sun
> and like the moon through all generations.
> They shall be like rain coming down on the fields,
> like showers watering the earth.
> Virtue shall flower in their days,

and world peace till the moon be no more.
May they rule from sea to sea,
and from the river to the ends of the earth....
They shall have pity for the needy and the poor;
they shall save the lives of the poor.
From oppression and violence they shall redeem them,
and precious shall their blood be.
To them, long life and continuous prayers;
day by day shall they be blessed.
May grain be in abundance on the earth,
and on the tops of the mountains
the crops shall rustle like Lebanon.
The city dwellers shall flourish
like the grass of the fields....
Blessed be Yahweh, the God of Israel,
who alone does wondrous deeds.
And blessed forever be God's glorious name;
may the whole earth be filled with God's glory.
Amen. Amen. (Psalm 72:1-8, 13-16, 18-19)

Although most psalms are credited to the poetic King David and his successor Solomon, the whole collection belongs to the people who sang and shaped them. Pinning down precise authorship is less important than knowing that an entire people has claimed the psalms as fitting prayer to the God of the Covenant and eventually to the God of Jesus.

The Psalms Are Poems to Ponder

Besides their obvious concern with human life and their ability to link people to one another in prayer, psalms gain power from their concrete and beautiful poetic style. Before anyone backs off at the mention of poetry, let me explain. I am referring to the use of imagery to convey insight.

Hebrew spirituality is not inclined to speak to God in terms of abstract doctrines. The psalms name God in a more tangible way than simply speaking of an almighty, all-knowing, supreme being. Although these qualities are also present, such abstract concepts do not feed our imaginations with portraits of God's mystery in experiential terms. Instead of using philosophical references, the psalms address God in true-to-life images—as a shepherd (Psalm 80) or a mighty fortress (Psalm 46)—instead of merely asserting that God is compassionate and righteous. The psalmist wants us to taste the goodness of Yahweh in as many flavors as possible. Vivid and artistic imagery helps fellow pray-ers to stay tuned in.

In a similar vein, psalmists never describe their own troubles in abstract terms. People are seldom philosophical when telling you about a grueling surgery or a grand vacation. My friends usually report concrete details in abundance so I can grasp how important the experience has been, just like any good storyteller and any good poet.

Since the psalmists are poetic storytellers, they use image after image to get the message across about their plights and pleasures. They want us to appreciate the scope of divine deeds on their behalf. They want to convey that it's not just any old problem that plagues them and that no other deity can respond adequately.

One psalm of woe describes ill-treatment by disloyal associates whose "malice oozes like grease;/their hearts overflow with schemes" (Psalm 73:7). Joy at having a good harvest and food on the table is depicted as "fields...arrayed with flocks/and the valleys blanketed with grain..." (Psalm 65:13). Another is concerned about growing old gracefully in the company of God: "bearing fruit in old age like trees full of sap—vigorous, widespreading..." (Psalm 92:14). Instead of accenting limits, this lyricist looks forward to ongoing development even in the aging process.

Poetry catches our attention by such vivid sketches of common human conditions. The assorted images highlight the mystery of both divine and human persons. Besides straight description, poems use metaphor, which focuses our awareness on particular aspects of meaning by speaking of one level of reality in terms of another reality, usually by comparing the two. In the passage from Psalm 92 cited above, aging trees and people are similar: Both are extended in time; both experience expansion as they grow old. In relationship to the Source of Life, however, the human being has infinitely more possibilities than the tree. Instead of saying, "Truth and beauty characterize human beings in everlasting relationship to God,"

9

the psalmic poet uses the shorthand method of metaphor, which delights our mind's eye with the color and freshness of trees. Reread the verse from Psalm 92 quoted above. Which is more inviting, the psalmist's metaphor or the abstract statement on truth and beauty?

Images like metaphors and symbols carry a *feeling* tone. You either feel comfortable or uncomfortable, excited or angry about the experience referred to by the image. Maybe you experience trees as reassuring signs of stability. Yet the very mention of old age may frighten you. If so, then the psalmist has given you something else to think and feel about. That is the strength of poetic language. It is especially effective for talking about God because we all have our own responses to deal with in that relationship. Images allow us to recognize and express our various understandings of God. (See pp. 45-46 for a related exercise.)

Like other poetry, the biblical psalm uses certain devices to connect us to the images and to connect image to image, line to line. Repetition is one such device. The recurrence of certain refrains—*Amen*, *Alleluia* and *Hosanna*—help everyone participate in the oral rendering of the prayer in keeping with its overall meaning.

Another common form of repetition involves one verse stating something and the next verse repeating the same thing in other words:

> O God, rescue me!
> the waters are up to my chin.
> I am wallowing in quicksand
> with no foothold for safety.
> I have slipped into deep water;
> the waves pound over me. (Psalm 69:1-2)

Each repetition strengthens and refines the preceding one. There is more than one way to get God's attention!

Exercise: Exploring the Psalms as Prayer

This chapter began with three people's impressions of the psalms. What is *your* impression? Does your answer have anything to do with prayer? Have you ever used the psalms in your personal prayer?

Thumb through the Book of Psalms and see how many of these prayers you can make your own right now. Write down the numbers of the psalms which most appeal to you. Watch for those psalms as you go on through this book.

2. The 'Nasty' Psalms

A Challenge for Christian Prayer

It is easy for me to be uplifted by psalms which use beautiful imagery. My shorthand name for these prayers of thanks and praise is the "nice" psalms. But then there are the "nasty" psalms. And the nastiest of them are why many people voice objections like these to praying the psalms: "They just show the Old Testament God of fear; I want to pray to a God of love," or, "How can Christians, who are supposed to love their enemies, pray out of a spirit of revenge?" or "Who needs those cursing psalms when we have so many beautiful Christian prayers?"

But what about a 70-year-old woman beaten bloodless by intruders, a school bus bombed by revolutionaries, Nazi brutality, a perjurer whose testimony sends an innocent man to death row? These inhumane behaviors cry to heaven for someone to give voice to the victims, to let the victims voice their agonizing anger. What, I ask myself, is so godly or Christian about denying judgment to cruelty and falsehood? These psalms acknowledge anger's spiritual power to transform unjust and hurtful situations.

Without a doubt the cursing psalms challenge the more timid among us with their vehemence. Psalm 140, for instance, calls a spade a spade by asking God to deal with evildoers:

> Let the mischief of their lips overwhelm them!
> Let burning coals fall upon them!
> Let them be cast into the fire, no more to rise!

...[Q]uickly let disaster hunt down the violent.
(Psalm 140:9-11)

Hebrew Spirituality in the 'Cursing' Psalms

To dismiss Old Testament spirituality as fear-filled, however, is a mistake. A quick check with the first five books of the Jewish Scriptures (the Torah) reveals that here is where Jesus learned the law of love which framed the parable on the Good Samaritan (see Luke 10:25-37). So predominant in Jewish prayer is the law of love that this commandment begins every synagogue or temple service to this day: "...[L]ove the LORD your God with all your heart, and with all your soul and with all your strength" (Deuteronomy 6:5).

The parallel command to love neighbor as self also comes from the Torah (Leviticus 19:17). And more than one Hebrew text refers to God as a mother (Psalm 131; Isaiah 49:14-17) or as a lover (Hosea 2:16-22). Jesus learned to address God as Father from the Jewish prayer tradition with which he had grown up (Psalm 103:1-5; Isaiah 63:15-16); in the Hebrew Scriptures the human Jesus discovered the tenderness of God.

Faith in God's compassion and human pity can give rise to the kind of curses found in the "nasty psalms." When we read of a man in a wheelchair shot in cold blood by terrorists or of the child abandoned by irresponsible parents, our hearts are moved. Sometimes we are even moved to a "By God, I'm going to do something about this!" Compassion stirs our sense of justice. We want to do right by the abused and neglected: And this is the sentiment behind the "nasty" psalms. This sampling from a series of Old Testament ritual curses expresses the same concern for justice:

> The Levites shall proclaim aloud to all the men of Israel: "Cursed be he who dishonors his father or his mother!" And all the people shall answer, "'Amen!'" "Cursed be he who moves his neighbor's landmarks!" And all the people shall answer, "Amen!" "Cursed be he who misleads a blind man on his way!" And all the people shall answer, "Amen!" "Cursed be he who violates the

14

rights of the alien, the orphan or the widow!" And all
the people shall answer, "Amen!"
"...Cursed be he who slays his neighbor in
secret!" And all the people shall answer, "Amen!"
"Cursed be he who accepts payment for slaying an
innocent man!" And all the people shall answer,
"Amen!" (Deuteronomy 27:14a-19, 24-25, NAB)

The God of the Covenant is the same God whom Jesus
reveals—a practical and realistic God whose curses are
motivated by justice and mercy. We partake of the divine heart
when we are similarly moved to do right for others. If we're
uncomfortable with emotions like anger, resentment and
revenge, so be it. Our discomfort cannot stop us from doing or
saying what is called for. And we can entrust our fiercest
feelings to the well-balanced deity of the Judeo-Christian
tradition. Psalmists know Yahweh is big enough to handle
outrage even when we are railing against God.

What better place to be yourself than in the presence of a
loving God? To feel free to express emotions with which we are
uncomfortable is a great sign of confidence in any relationship.
To let God know about our fury and alarm is an
acknowledgement of the divine ability to accept us as we are.

At times the psalmist simultaneously displays anger and
impatience toward God while spewing curses at the
perpetrators of evil. Instead of hiding these vengeful thoughts
and emotions, the psalmist shows trust in God by fully
exposing personal outrage.

Whoever is behind Psalm 35 is terribly fearful of losing a
court case to liars. Occurring in the context of prayer, the curses
help the psalmist put the outcome of the trial into Yahweh's
hands. Under the same circumstances, I suspect a lot of us
could pray equally vehemently if only we dared:

And for those who are out to kill me:
disgrace, dishonor, and ruin.
Drive back, confound, and confuse
those who plot my fall.
May they be like chaff before the wind,
with the angel of Yahweh to chase them.

Let their path be dark and dangerous,
with the angel of Yahweh to goad them. (Psalm 35:4-6)

In these verses the psalmist is only asking that the liars be tormented by their consciences. But he continues, making it clear that people he has befriended have set him up and double-crossed him:

Perjurers take the stand,
charging me with deeds I know nothing about.
They repay my charity with evil.
My soul grieves. (Psalm 35:11-12)

To make matters worse, strangers hear the falsehoods and join his opponents:

Complete strangers
rip me to pieces with shouts,
ridiculing me with their taunts,
grinding their teeth at me. (Psalm 35:15b-16)

At his wit's end, he clamors:

Yahweh, how much longer will you allow this?
Save my soul from these beasts,
my only life from these lions.
I will give thanks in the Great Assembly,
glorifying you where the people meet. (Psalm 35:17-18)

Before the psalm ends the victim calls God to account, then rests the case with Yahweh:

You have seen, Yahweh.
Do not be silent.
Do not be far from me!
Awake! Defend me!
Side with me, my God.
Yahweh, you are just, so do justice for me.
Do not let them gloat over me. (Psalm 35:22-24)

Any of us who has ever been the target of malicious gossip, let alone a court case, can identify with that woeful helplessness. To strip the sufferer of the freedom to speak to God, the one last hope for an honest hearing, would be more oppressive than the curses themselves.

Jesus' 'Nastiness'

Jesus was no wimp when it came to venting ire toward perpetrators of injustice and harmful hypocrisy; he hurled curses in no uncertain terms. Matthew, who is interested in the establishment of a genuine Judeo-Christian community, writes that Jesus rejected untrue disciples with the harsh words of Psalm 6:8: "Out of my sight, you evildoers!" (7:23b, NAB). Luke, the evangelist who tries to be as inclusive as possible, presents a barrage of reproaches from Jesus toward unscrupulous leaders of religious and legal circles:

> You Pharisees! You cleanse the outside of cup and dish, but within you are filled with rapaciousness and evil. Fools! Did not he who made the outside make the inside too?... Woe to you Pharisees! You pay tithes on mint and rue and all the garden plants, while negelecting justice and the love of God.... Woe to you Pharisees! You love the front seats in synagogues and marks of respect in public. Woe to you! You are like hidden tombs over which men walk unawares....
> Woe to you lawyers also! You lay impossible burdens on men but will not lift a finger to lighten them. Woe to you! You build the tombs of the prophets, but it was your fathers who murdered them. You show that you stand behind the deeds of your fathers: they committed the murders and you erect the tombs....
> Woe to you lawyers! You have taken away the key of knowledge. You yourselves have not gained access, yet you have stopped those who wished to enter!
> (Luke 11:39, 42a, 43-44, 46-48, 52, NAB)

And the manipulation of others' minds and resources goads Jesus into an open condemnation of unprofessional scribes

17

according to Mark's succinct report (12:38-40).

In another scene Jesus upsets tables of moneychangers and calls them uncomplimentary names (John 2:13-17). No wonder they dub him a troublemaker later on (John 7:11-13). Jesus also quotes Psalm 41:10 at the Last Supper, in recognition of the sin of betrayal:

"He who partook of bread with me
has raised his heel against me." (John 13:18, NAB)

From the cross Jesus reproaches his Father with Psalm 22:2: "My God, my God, why have you forsaken me?" (Matthew 27:46b, NAB). At the lowest point of his Passion, Jesus entrusted God with the depth of his disappointment. He relied on his Father even as he seemed to point out God's failure at that particular juncture when the Resurrection was still beyond view. Like us, Jesus prayed out of the reality of his immediate situation, which called for something more than mere politeness. Besides, he knew God is big enough to take in an honest appeal, whether it sounds acceptable to human ears or not. Jesus was honest, and the psalm fit his honesty.

His sinless mother knew that God can wreak havoc with human conventions. In the course of her canticle of praise, the Magnificat, she incorporates verses from Psalms 113, 75 and 107 to portray the Mighty One toppling the rich and powerful (Luke 1:52-54). Why does a mild-mannered Mary choose to cite these verses of upheaval even at a time of joy? Probably because of her sense of Yahweh as a decisive God who wants to take the action necessary to transform helplessness into strength. I am glad that her Son learned how to pray in a down-to-earth fashion from this Jewish mother.

Without the credentials of Mary or Jesus, we may fear to pray in any manner that smacks of judgmental or violent attitudes. What's safe for the holy may not be safe for us! Moreover, we have been taught to refrain from judging lest we be judged, to forgive as we have been forgiven and, more recently, that nonviolence is a mandate of the gospel. If we accept these teachings at face value, our only recourse is to pray tamely, it seems. With judgment branded as uncharitable and violence as immoral, it is understandable that some portions of psalmody pose a dilemma.

A Helpful Distinction

I find it helpful to distinquish between judgment in a *moral* sense and judgment in a *behavioral* sense. Of course we must refrain from judging the innermost conscience of other human beings. It is beyond our capability to assess the inner worth of any person or condemn a person as unfit for God's presence. We are expected, however, to make judgments about the effects of someone's action when it clearly affects another.

In other words, I can suspend moral judgment on the professor who intimidates a female student with sexual innuendo. The man may not know any better; he may not be capable of anything morally better. I don't know what wounds he carries from his childhood to evoke his dastardly behavior.

But I do know the effects are troubling to the student. I am called upon to evaluate the harmful effects and do what I can to alleviate the situation. It may require that I speak out. I am morally bound in my realm of responsibility to exercise that kind of judgment.

In such a crisis I may be moved to pray in a way that storms heaven. Psalm 36 would work just fine in this instance. It flatly recognizes that some people hold values different from those I associate with a God of the living. I can pray in the place of the frightened student:

> Sin speaks to sinners
> in the depths of their hearts.
> No awe of God is before their eyes.
> They so flatter themselves
> that they do not know their guilt.
> In their mouths are lies and foolishness.
> Gone is all wisdom.
> They plot the downfall of goodness
> as they lie on their beds.
> They set their feet on evil ways,
> they hold to what is evil.
> Your love, Yahweh, reaches to heaven;
> your faithfulness to the skies.

19

Your justice is like a mountain—
your judgments like the deep.
To all creation you give protection.
Your people find refuge
in the shelter of your wings.
They feast on the riches of your house;
they drink from the stream of your delight.
You are the source of life,
and in your light we see light.
Continue your love to those who know you,
doing justice to the upright in heart.
Let the foot of the proud not crush me,
nor the hand of the wicked drive me away.
See how the evildoers have fallen!
Flung down, they shall never rise. (Psalm 36:1-12)

Perhaps the sinners in the psalm indeed have no fear of
God because they have neither knowledge of nor room for the
psalmist's God in their hearts. People who espouse values
different from those of Yahweh's people through both
circumstance and choice may be sincere but misguided. There
is a difference, however, between sincerity and accuracy. God
judges us for the former, but calls us to assess the abusive
situation accurately and, at least, to pray on behalf of the victim.

When We Are Victims

Once when I myself was the victim of blatant injustice, I
found it more than helpful to create my own "Psalm of Disgust":

Help me, Lord, I am chewing my nails
and spitting them out in rage.
You yourself tasted the degrading dish I was served,
and the cup of tears I was given to drink.
You know I was innocent of those charges
trumped up in Johnny-come-lately style.
Like a victim I started to swallow it all
but now I'm fed up with their cruelty and cowardice.
It's no longer a secret how harshly they acted,
tossing me out like a piece of garbage.

20

Civilized people call it barbaric,
   but clamors for restitution fall on Neanderthal ears.
Can't those evildoers see that their institutional idols
   grind away at your creative Spirit?
With their small weak egos they have decreed:
   It's expedient that one woman die this year
   for the sake of unprofessional administrators.

Feebly they question each other
   and rationalize to save face.
   Let these cave men pick each other to the bone.
They feed on their precious chain of command,
   let their anxiety gnaw at them from here on in.

Lord of Justice, like you I want to vomit
   these lukewarm officials out of my mouth,
I can't really stomach them any more.

Now it is up to you, my God,
   to seat me at other tables of employment.
Then I will praise you for a menu
   which nourishes me with your goodness
   and opportunities à la carte.

Let me pray on.

You are no stranger, God of the Little People,
to the way that humans can hurt one another even
in the name of heaven. Just as Your Son Jesus
suffered at the hands of mean people without
becoming mean or bitter himself, help me hang on
to what is important, so that I can continue to
live by his Spirit. I ask this in his name. Amen.

It has surprised me how readily other people can identify
with my psalm. Some who publicly advocate nonviolence
affirm the hiss of the text. Words can certainly be violent, but
words *used in prayer* are a nonviolent weapon.

I was quite aware of my capacity for violence in the
"Psalm of Disgust," but by being aware of it and turning the
situation over to God, I was less likely to let my feelings control
my behavior. My psalmic expression gives due attention to my
strong emotions and still fulfills the oft-quoted line,

"'Vengeance is mine; I will repay,' says the Lord" (Romans 12:19, NAB). All I ask is for God to do justice for me. God's judgment can only be rendered by God; Christ's peace can only be given by Christ. In the meantime I cannot act as if nothing evil was perpetrated, whether it was I or someone else who was the target.

Before I leave the subject of violence, let me clarify that nonviolence is not an absolute. It may be an ideal, but it can also be an escape from responsibility. Physical violence may not be the preferred way to respond to an evil, but it need not be totally struck from consideration.

Speaking in the name of common sense, in good conscience and in an effort to come to terms with the whole of my religious tradition, I find it inconceivable that my brother would stand by and watch a rapist attack his young daughter. He would never forgive himself if he did not intervene physically to prevent the molestation.

The principle, then, is this: Christians use what is needed to transform the situation, particularly where helpless victims are involved. If the gravity of the context admits no other workable alternative, violence is not to be automatically dismissed. Much less should praying out of an awareness of violent emotions be dismissed.

Exercise: Approaching the 'Nasty Psalms'

Some readers may still have trouble praying the rough stuff of the cursing psalms. The following four suggestions offer alternate ways to pray the psalms.

1) Select.

Simply choose the parts of the psalter that correspond to your spirituality. At times this means choosing only those psalms which omit cursing, especially if you do not want to offend the ears and sensibilities of a community. Concentrate on the psalms of praise and of trust (see Chapters Four and Six). As for the laments, stick to the penitential texts like Psalms 6,

30, 51 and 130 or to Psalms 17, 26, 44, 88 and similar psalms (see Chapter Five).

Another way to select is to edit. If most of a psalm appeals to you but some verses are disconcerting, then omit the troublesome sections to salvage the rest for prayer. Keep the whole psalm on file, however, because something may happen in the future which calls for such energetic verses!

2) Reinterpret.

The psalms can be very graphic in the plight they call down on their enemies. For example:

> O daughter of Babylon—you destroyer—
> happy those who shall repay you
> the evil you have done us!
> Happy those who shall seize and smash
> your little ones against the rock! (Psalm 137:8-9)

Suppose this is not a later addition by extraneous sources, as some commentators hold. Suppose the captives really prayed this way. If we are unable to enter into the plight of the Jewish people in captivity, bemoaning their exile and attempting to fight back with prayers, their sole weapons, we can reinterpret. We can imagine that Babylon stands for evil personified. In the analogy, Babylon then becomes the parent of its offspring, namely the horrible treatment it perpetuates. The babes or little ones can then be understood as the fruits of this enemy's wickedness, which Israel wants not only to resist but to stamp out decisively.

Try praying the whole psalm with this in mind:

> By the rivers of Babylon
> we sat and wept, remembering Zion.
> On the poplars of the land
> we hung up our harps;
> there our captors asked of us
> the lyrics of our songs
> and urged us to be joyous:
> "Sing for us one of the songs of Zion!" they said.

How could we sing a song of Yahweh
while in a foreign land?
If I forget you, Jerusalem,
may my right hand forget its skill!
May my tongue cleave to the roof of my mouth
if I forget you,
if I do not consider Jerusalem
my greatest joy.

Remember, Yahweh, what the Edomites did
that day in Jerusalem.
When they said, "Tear it down,
tear it down to its foundations!"
O daughter of Babylon—you destroyer—
happy those who shall repay you
the evil you have done us!
Happy those who shall seize and smash
your little ones against the rock! (Psalm 137:1-9)

Another form of reinterpretation is to recognize the hyperbole, or exaggeration, which Middle East literature often uses to highlight what is at stake. By building up its point, the prayer builds up its poignancy and makes a claim on God to save the Chosen People from terrible fate. Psalm 59, for example, obviously exaggerates in comparing traitors to dogs:

At night they slink back like wild dogs,
roaming the town and howling.
Their tongues drip blasphemy,
and their mouths are filled with insults.
"After all," they snap, "who will hear us?"
(Psalm 59:6-7)

All that dramatic imagery about mongrels is preparing for the strongest appeal the psalmist can make to persuade God to do justice:

"But you, God, will laugh at them.
You make light of all the nations." (Psalms 59:8)

The goal is to put the adversaries in perspective in comparison to the power and righteousness of Yahweh.

3) Rewrite.

Harsh images soften when translated into a contemporary setting and language. Some contemporary authors have attempted such recomposition, producing a beautiful blend of the original's main dynamic with modern overtones. Pray, for instance, this version of Psalm 43 by Francis Patrick Sullivan:

> God, argue for me against them,
> get me free! They believe
> nothing, they trick You, profane You!
> Why throw me away, You,
> my one defense, God, why let them
> threaten my life with death.
> Brighten it instead with Your truth!
> Lead me up the mountain
> to Your holy place. I could walk
> right in to Your altar,
> my God, my joy, my life. I could
> take a harp, make it sing
> to You, God, my God! You, my soul,
> why so sad, why breathe it
> at me? Wait! I can still cherish
> my God, my freedom here!

4) Reread.

Some people find in a closer reading that the psalmist is, for example, only quoting another person's curses and reporting them to Yahweh to let God know how serious the situation is. This sort of discovery often occurs in psalms which depict someone falsely accused; what the psalmist reports is the accusations and curses by others (see, for example, Psalm 109:6-19).

Rereading other psalms will reveal that what at first sounds like a curse is simply a prediction of what will happen if the wicked keep on doing evil. It is the old story of the bad tree bearing bad fruit. It is like the parent who says to the child, "If you take drugs, you will be subject to traumas you've never dreamed of, and your family will not know how to deal with you. You will lose control over your life and you will suffer immensely." In other words, the curses of Psalm 5 might be reread in the future tense: If you continue to reject Yahweh, this is what you can expect. You will bring it on yourself. If the liars continue lying, they will reap what they sow and:

> ...fall by their own devices
> and be cast out because they have rebelled against God.
>
> (See Psalm 5:10-12)

A Last Word

After all is said and done, I see a value in retaining the "nasty" psalms as a healthy way to pray through anger and to *use* anger in God's presence to ask for more enduring efforts—if not in your lifetime or mine, then in God's time. So, ladies and gentlemen—and I use that form of address advisedly—I dare you to pray the psalms!

3. Jumbled Prayer

Making Sense of the Psalter

The psalms emerged out of the experiences of people who lived life to the full. These prayers therefore reflect the jumble of human experience. One day we can be extraordinarily pleased about how well the children are doing in school; the next, one of them is hospitalized and we are lost to anxiety. Sometimes the psalms remind me of the stock market: quick shifts from despondency to confidence and back again.

My first encounters with the inconsistency in these old oral prayers swiftly brought me to realize that they did not originate in some academic outline; they reflect real human mood swings. From moment to moment they change because of indecisiveness or because of new information—just as we change our minds. The psalms of lament, for instance, accent doubt in the midst of trouble. We could raise similar questions: "How long, O God, before you do something to cure me?" "Have you even noticed the way other countries are mocking our nation?" "How can you save me when my sin is so great?" Then all of a sudden the tide turns and waves of confidence wash over the crisis: "O God, you have come to my rescue in the past and will do so again." "You did promise to be with your people, and we are depending on your promise and your steadfast love." "I don't know exactly how you will do it, God, but I can already see you have the wisdom to end my/our troubles." Such alternations between doubt and faith continue to accompany upheavals in our lives.

The psalms are jumbled prayer because they are full of

human life. Psalm 43 demonstrates in five short verses how many moods can coexist in a single prayer. Trace the verse-by-verse progression from panic to doubt to confidence to anticipated joy to hope:

> Do me justice, O God, and plead my cause
> against a faithless people;
> from the deceitful and unjust, rescue me.
> For you, O God, are my stronghold.
> Why do you keep me so far away?
> Why must I go about in mourning,
> oppressed by the enemy?
> Send forth your light and your truth—
> they shall guide me;
> let them bring me to your holy mountain,
> to your dwelling place.
> Then will I go in to the altar of God, the God of my
> delight and joy;
> Then will I praise you with the harp,
> O God, my God!
> Why are you so downcast, O my soul?
> Why do you sigh within me?
> Put your hope in God,
> For I shall again be thankful
> in the presence of my savior and my God.
>
> (Psalm 43:1-5)

Psalms Are Oral Prayer

The fact that the psalms were originally *oral* prayer cannot be underestimated. Remember that psalms are first and foremost poetry (see pp. 8-10), and poetry is sensitive to the sounds of the language. Just as Shakespeare's moving narratives were not delivered in writing but in song and speech, psalms are quite an earful, quite a mouthful. They sprang up long before the written word, about 1,000 years before Jesus. They were kept alive as oral prayer for 500 years or more before psalmic compositions appeared in writing for the community (not counting the ones some eager beavers scrawled on temple walls).

Oral prayer was the primary medium for both praising and petitioning the God of David, Hannah, Deborah and Solomon. Whether God's people were exiled in a foreign country (Psalm 137) or ecstatic at home again (Psalm 126), they sounded off in the presence of Yahweh and one another. When King David sang aloud, confessing his sin and asking for forgiveness, God wasn't the only one who was listening and responding to the penitent.

Psalmic prayer became part of the people's living memory because ritual elements made them memorable. Melodies reinforced the words; lyre and harp strengthened the melodies. Various settings invited communal vocal participation; in the dialogues in Psalms 24 and 124, for example, the worshipers, are called upon to answer the priest's questions. (A similar ritual dialogue is the question-and-answer format of renewing baptismal promises).

In addition, acclamations like *Alleluia, Hosanna* and *Amen* are sprinkled throughout the psalter (see psalms 105, 113 and 72). Psalm 136 is a kind of litany with the recurrent phrase, "Your love is everlasting," sung by the congregation, a form which clearly indicates a context of public worship.

The free association of feelings and events is another characteristic of oral expression. Listen as a fisherman tells of the one that got away. While recounting the sad disappearance of the giant fins, the storyteller may suddenly delight in a detail about "what a beauty that one was, glinting in the sun as it waved good-bye!" The story's sentiments move back and forth naturally from disappointment to fondness for the fish as a friend passing through the fisherman's life.

This kind of speaking requires the listener to be alert to the shifts and to live through them with the one giving the account. Tears and laughter readily mingle as speaker and listener grow closer. What first looks like a jumble is actually a *mingling*. Rarely do we limit our thoughts or schedule our emotions in live conversation. And that is what the psalms are: a live conversation with God in the midst of the gathering.

The effect of oral prayer is that everyone hears the story at the same time. It is easier to close your eyes to block out sights than your ears to block out sounds. Willing or not, someone with ear plugs in the presence of a rock band will experience at least the physical impact of the rhythmic sound waves. People listening together become aware of one another more quickly, which leads to a greater sense of unity than the printed medium can create.

The pray-er, in this case the psalmist, looses God's dynamic Word into the midst of an attentive assembly. They may grab it or be grabbed by it; they may change it or be changed by it as it becomes their collective own. Over time they either accept it as true to their community's experience or reject it as inappropriate. Not only is it a risky venture to pray to the living God; it is even riskier to pray among one's fellow believers. It's the difference between a movie and a live drama.

Thank heavens the People of God have risked it. No longer do these oral prayers belong only to David or some other bard. Because the psalmists were willing to share their encounters with Yahweh, we benefit from the outpourings of their hearts.

Only within the last few centuries did it become common to use the psalms for private prayer. Not until then could the printing press produce enough affordable, individual copies. Texts which can be read with one's own eyes tend to get privatized; it doesn't matter whether others are interested at the moment or not. The printed page gives the reader more control over his or her response. It's the difference between reading a letter and talking with someone face-to-face.

The biblical psalms, whether individually or communally prayed, presuppose a God who listens, who responds and who becomes part of our story. Again we glimpse the distinctiveness of the One whose care Jesus personally testified to, and the One he counted on to be here for us.

In private as well as public worship, the God of the covenant and the God of Jesus still hears us singing our hearts out in jubilation and invocation. How can this God resist the familiar sound of people who have been inspired to stay in touch with the Holy One who has decided to stay in touch with us all these millennia?

Arranging and Rearranging the Psalms

The need for order is basic to human beings. The perception of order seems to satisfy our yearning to make sense of our lives. My desk and my kitchen cabinets may be arranged differently from my neighbor's, but both of us depend on knowing where the papers or spices are when we want them. In relationships, we count on certain patterns of communication with primary people in family or business. The spouse who gets a daily phone call from the other partner during lunchtime will probably get anxious if, on a routine day, there has been no contact by late afternoon. We tend to proceed with our lives on the basis of the order we understand to be at work in them.

Disorder is not unmanageable, but it poses a challenge wherever we find it. Even if our ordering is purely mental (imagining what could have happened to prevent the spouse's daily phone call), we zero in on reality and rearrange, if possible, the parts that don't fit. When that fails, we call an item or event puzzling, taking comfort in the order we achieve just by labeling it puzzling. We must put things in their place, if only in our mind's place, in order to function day by day.

This fundamental urge to order has given rise to many attempts to categorize the psalms.

In ancient Israel someone divided the psalter into five smaller "books": (I) 1-41; (II) 42-72; (III) 73-89; (IV) 90-106; and (V) 107-150. These divisions may indicate a development in the people's understanding of God at different periods of their history or perhaps the supposed identity of their authors—David, Solomon or others. Or the division may be imposed simply to imitate the Torah, the first five books of the Hebrew Scripture.

Other more understandable divisions exist in the psalter. One entire subset of psalms is dubbed "Pilgrimage Psalms" by scholars (Psalms 120-134), who suspect they were sung on the annual trip to the Jerusalem temple during the high holy days. (In Luke's Gospel, the boy Jesus got lost on one such trip.) Within this subset are psalms of trust (Psalms 121, 124), a penitential lament (Psalm 130), and at least one psalm of thanksgiving (Psalm 126), not to mention the night prayer (Psalm 134) which concludes this section of the psalter.

Modern commentators differ on methods of classification. Some equate psalms of *lament* with prayers of *supplication*. A subgroup of praise psalms may be called *royal* psalms by one scholar and *messianic* psalms by another—and both may disagree about whether Psalm 118 belongs in either category or should instead be called an *enthronement* psalm. One author groups the *wisdom* psalms (which depict God as guide and lawgiver) separately; elsewhere they comprise a category of *didactic* psalms. (Both *didactic* and *wisdom* connote prayers that deal with the fine art of practical living, see Chapter Seven.)

For the purpose of this book, I use three generally accepted classes of psalms: psalms of *praise*, of *lament* and of *trust*. When I go to pray them, I am frankly more concerned about how they can help me understand and cope with life than in what exact category they fall.

An individual psalm may not fit precisely into only one category anyway. Spontaneous movement from anxious laments to confident thanks creates the most common example of a cross-category psalm. Compare Psalm 61:1-2 with Psalm 61:9-10.

Psalms remain as varied as life itself, despite our attempts to group them. The people who composed and prayed the psalms understood that no human concern is too large or too small for God's attention. From wanting to get a good night's sleep (Psalm 4) to praying for the arrival of the messianic reign (Psalm 72), the people depend on the relationship into which Yahweh has called them. Given that basic fact, their prayer could be as dappled as their lives demanded because humanity was and is God's priority.

Exercise: Dwelling On a Psalm

Rather than attempting to put the psalms into some order, find your place in the disorder. The suggestions offered are highly subjective—for where can we start if not with the individuals that we are?

The first method for discovering how a given psalm can speak to your heart is influenced by the Benedictine tradition of sacred reading (*lectio divina*). It emphasizes the process of letting a word or phrase in the Scripture speak to your own sense of meaning. In this approach to meditation, you simply read a psalm slowly, reflectively—until something catches your attention. Then you stay with that piece, letting it bring you into touch with your own mystery and God's mystery in you. Let your reflection lead you where it will: to feelings, to insights, or to inspirations for turning some aspect of your life over to God in a fuller measure. After "chewing on God's Word," as one monastic writer phrased it, you give thanks for the nourishment and move on until another passage speaks to your heart. You are not expected to finish any given number of verses; in fact, you may return to the same passage every day for as long as it continues to hold your attention to God's presence.

Another way to dwell on one psalm is to pray it in several translations. Thus you extend the dialogue with the Word; its fullness is rounded out by the other versions.

In reading and rereading a translation of a given psalm in your Bible, underline or highlight the words and phrases that lead you into reflection which engage your heart. Then do the same with a translation of the same psalm from at least one other source.

Instead of reading the Word per se, you are letting the Word read you. You are being called into a growing knowledge and responsiveness to the God of the Bible. This personalized dwelling on a psalm characterizes contemporary approaches to prayer. It also prepares the individual who takes part in group prayer of any sort to share faith with others based on the interactions with the texts.

A psalm with universal appeal is the Good Shepherd Psalm. Of all the psalms, this one has probably been translated and paraphrased more than any other. I have seen a version which related to a political figure and another in the form of a prayer for a dieter. Review a standard translation of Psalm 23—perhaps listen to a musical setting of it—and then explore the additional translations below. Enjoy dwelling on this well-loved prayer.

An Eskimo Version*

The Lord is my master: I am his dog.
He makes me lie down in soft snow;
He leads me across firm ice:
He calls to me encouragingly.
He drives me on good trails because I belong to Him.
Through storms and troubles, I will not be afraid
    because He is with me,
My harness is securely fastened
And his hand is on the sled.
He guards me while I eat, though enemies lurk near.
He doctors my hurts.
My heart overflows with gratitude.
Only kindness and gentle care will be mine from the
    hands of this master
And I will be on his team forever. (Author Unknown)

A Contemporary Jewish Version

The Lord is my shepherd
and keeps me from wanting
what I can't have
Lush green grass is set
around me and crystal water
to graze by
There I revive with my soul
find the way that love makes
for His name
and though I pass through cities of pain,
through death's living shadow
I'm not afraid to touch
to know who I am
Your shepherd's staff is always there
to keep me calm
in my body

---

* The Eskimo knows nothing of sheep. To tell an Eskimo these truths,
you must use the dog, which is almost a part of an Eskimo's family.

You set a table before me
in the presence of my enemies
you give me grace to speak
to quiet them
to be full with humanness
to be warm in my soul's lightness
to feel contact every day
in my hand and in my belly
love coming down to me
in the air of your name, Lord,
in your house
in my life. (From *Blues of the Sky*, by David Rosenberg)

A Cherokee Indian Version

The Great Father above a Shepherd Chief is, I am His
and with Him I want not.
He throws out to me a rope, and the name of the rope
is love, and He draws me, and he draws me into a
good road. His name is wonderful.
Sometime, it may be very soon, it may be longer, it may
be long, long time, He will draw me into a place
between mountains. It is dark here, but I'll draw back
not. I'll be afraid not, for it is in there between those
mountains that the Shepherd Chief wills me, and the
hunger I have felt in my heart all through this life will
be satisfied.
Sometimes He makes the rope into a whip, but
afterwards He gives me a staff to lean on.
He spreads a table before me with all kinds of food. He
puts His hand upon my head, and all the "tired" is
gone. My cup He fills till it runs over.
What I tell you is true. I lie not. These roads that are
"away ahead" will stay with me through this life, and
afterwards I will go to live in the "Big Teepee" and sit
down with the Shepherd Chief forever.
(From *The Bible Reader: An Interfaith Interpretation*)

You could also try dwelling on the two versions of Psalm
43 in this book (see pp. 25 and 28), since they are taken from

35

two distinct collections. One comes from *Half a Psalter* by Francis Sullivan, who carefully brings out the psalm's lyrical qualities and imagery. The other is taken from an edition by two Franciscan sisters interested in removing gender-biased language. An annotated list of psalm translations in Appendix B offers further guidance on possible versions for helping you dwell on a psalm.

As you reflect on whatever draws you in either or both versions, ask yourself if there is any pattern. Become conscious of what attracts you. Is there an image which disturbs or agrees with your idea of God, yourself, other human beings? Does the psalm express a particular view of the world? What could this indicate about your relationship with God? Respond in prayer appropriate to what is happening in your life right now.

Dwelling on a psalm, either as an individual piece or as a series of several translations, can become part of spiritual journal-keeping. Over time, the notes and emphases you focus on can be used to indicate recurrent concerns in your prayer—especially if you ask yourself in each entry, "What is going on in my life right now that would lead me to notice that particular phrase? Where is my energy going? Do I want it to go in that direction? How does my interest connect with the God of the psalms, my God?"

4. If You're Willing to Wonder

Psalms of Praise

Praise and thanksgiving appear in almost every psalm. Sometimes the entire poem is devoted to tones of blessing. Psalm 117's two verses, for instance, burst with joy and summon other nations to do likewise:

> Alleluia!
> Praise Yahweh, all you nations,
> glorify Yahweh all you peoples
> for God's love is strong,
> God's faithfulness eternal.

At other times a single snatch of praise emerges in the middle of a lament or erupts during a psalm expressing confidence in God's love during distress. The next chapter will treat the psalms of lament; this one focuses on the "psalms of wonder," the psalms of praise.

Wonder, blessing, praise and thanksgiving are all virtually the same in psalmody; they are highly *active* responses to God's enduring love. When we are awestruck at the "sweet mystery of life," we are likely to feel a rush of gratitude. Saying it aloud increases our own and others' awareness.

Our appreciation often takes the form of wanting to do something creative for someone else—make a donation, light a votive candle, take someone to lunch—just because life is so good we want to share it. Action-oriented thanks can be seen in the child who receives a bike for Christmas. A conventional "thanks" is fine but there's extra satisfaction when the receiver pedals around exclaiming, "Look, everybody! It's awesome! Watch me break the Olympic record!"

Psalmists express their thanks with that same sort of exuberance and abandon. They stand up and proclaim:

> All you peoples, clap your hands;
> raise a joyful shout to God.
> For the Most High is awesome,
> glorious over all earth.
> God subdues peoples under us.
> The God of Love chooses for us our inheritance...
> and rules over all the nations...." (Psalm 47:1-4, 8)

Actively giving thanks in the presence of others is a sure way to multiply praise for the one who made this experience possible. Telling others of divine deeds is a life-giving way to say thanks because it stimulates others' sense of the goodness of life. Also, when we live in a spirit of praise, we bless God for all the goodness shown to us in creation, redemption and, finally, the Kingdom.

Those three theological themes—creation, redemption and Kingdom—depict what God does for us. But how do these major themes translate into human experience so that we know we have something to sing about?

I call these moments *understanding*, *fulfillment* and *encouragement*. They are three gracious reasons for praising God.

Understanding

Knowing that we are related to God, other people and the rest of the universe grounds our understanding of our whole and holy identity. In a lifetime, it is no small matter to glimpse the dimensions of our totality: who we are down deep, where we came from and where we are going in life.

Several psalms celebrate this sense among the People of God. Historical psalms such as Psalm 107 tell their story, singing about the divine loving-kindness and fidelity intertwined with their history. Accounts of national victories and close calls evoke praise from the faithful and understanding people who pray Psalm 48. In Psalm 104, understanding turns to pure joy because the Creator cares about feeding the birds of the air as well as two-footed human beings who, in Psalm 8, approach divine splendor.

The psalms are filled with wonder at the original connection of creation (Psalm 148); at the ongoing touch of redemption (Psalm 99); at the promise of a universal reign of justice personified (Psalm 98). These themes of creation, redemption (or salvation) and the future Kingdom recur in the psalter. All three are secured by God's promise.

Psalm 100, a well-worn, often-sung selection, reflects biblical wonder at being creatures in a sustained relationship to God. Yahweh's ongoing concern is cast in a comforting shepherd image. Take a deep breath and let yourself—your many selves—be in the presence of the One who loves you as you pray this psalm:

> Shout for joy to God,
> all the lands!
> Serve God with gladness!
> Come into God's presence with joyful singing!
> Know that Yahweh is God!
> Yahweh made us, and we belong to God;
> we are God's people and the sheep of God's pasture.
> Enter God's gates with thanksgiving
> and the courts with praise!
> Give thanks to God, bless God's name!
> For Yahweh is good;
> God's steadfast love endures forever,
> and God's faithfulness to all generations.
>
> (Psalm 100:1-5)

From time to time I write my own psalms or my spinoffs from the originals. In the prayer below, I understand my relationship to God in the context of the person of Jesus. Like Psalm 100, "A Psalm in Praise of Life's Journey" moves into his loving presence:

> Hear ye, hear ye, all you pilgrim people!
> Rise up quickly, follow our Lord and Leader:

He goes before us into Galilee
and other strange lands as yet still unknown.

Praise Jesus who walks before us.

The firstborn of our number goes before us
in the name of our God
who knows all our comings and our goings,
all our sittings and our standings.

Praise Jesus who walks beside us.

And so, all you pilgrim people, rise up
in the name of Love, whose movements
make the heart restless but steady the feet,
for Love has its come, Love has its go.

Praise Jesus who walks beside us.

Yes, come to the Light, the Water, the Way—
to the Word, the Body, the Bread.
Later we will speak of go but as for now,
come, all you pilgrim people, rise up!

Praise God!

Fulfillment

Experiences of fulfillment never stay around long enough to suit me. They are the stuff happy memories are made of when you look back and think, "Yes, it was all worth it."

Thomas Aquinas outlined what I mean by experiences of fulfillment when he wrote about the qualities of beauty. We know something is beautiful (not just pretty, which is more superficial) when our appreciation includes a fourfold response: (1) a sense of being strengthened; (2) a sense of being cleansed or made better; (3) a sense of order or harmony; (4) an element of surprise at how well things work together to produce a sense of goodness which is not entirely in our control. The four responses can occur in any order but happen more or less at the same time so that one has the sense of their unity rather than their separateness.

Indeed, I can get enthusiastic over the depth and breadth

of a beautiful experience. And the word *enthusiasm* is accurate because at root it means "filled with God." A fulfilling experience is one that is beautiful, filled with God in my awareness; it is strengthening, surprising, harmonious with my innards and transforming of my life. Enthusiasm fits.

Some experiences commonly associated with fulfillment are birthing or adopting a child, winning a valuable prize, waking up so refreshed you "feel human again," receiving applause, finishing a job to your satisfaction, making a freeing decision or appreciating something—a ballet, a sunset—which is so beautiful it makes you feel like bursting at the seams.

Psalms which speak to the experience of fulfillment are hymns of praise—like the glorious Psalm 150, which almost explodes with praise of God's splendor and majesty. To get the full blast of these hymns, turn a stereo up loud enough to hear all the power of the percussion section and let the the violins swirl around you as you read.

> Alleluia!
> Praise to you, Yahweh, in your sanctuary!
> Praise to you in the firmament of your strength.
> Praise you for your mighty deeds;
> praise you for your sovereign majesty.
> Praise to you, Yahweh, with the blast of the trumpet,
> praise with lyre and harp.
> Praise with timbrel and dance,
> praise with strings and flutes.
> Praise to you, Yahweh, with resounding cymbals.
> Let everything that has breath praise Yahweh.
> Alleluia. (Psalm 150:1-6)

Encouragement

A third reason to give praise is encouragement. It happens when we affirm with the God of Genesis that life is thoroughly good—not only now but on into the future. It needs our enthusiasm. At the risk of sounding trite, I refer to the spirit of the rousing camp song, "If you're happy and you know it/And you really want to show it,/Clap your hands!" Instead of stomping feet or clapping, the psalmist shows it by singing and sharing praise. You might consider the psalmists the cheerleaders of life and goodness. They invite you, me and any bystander to become their prayer partners by singing over and over a response such as "Your love is everlasting" (Psalm 136) to flesh out a litany of praise for each of God's works. The marvels range from setting the earth on the waters to rescuing the Hebrews from the Pharaoh.

There are a couple of ways that psalmody cheers life on. One way is found in the "wisdom psalms." The entire Book of Psalms is usually classified as wisdom literature, but some psalms deal more directly with practical living. In the longest biblical psalm, Psalm 119 (with 176 verses!), every stanza applauds the divine Law as a wise way to cultivate the goodness of life. Practicing virtues like truth, reverence and making the right choices leads to life rather than death. Psalm 1 drives the same point home. Psalms that promote practical virtues urge life to continue through proper channels.

Another way the psalmist encourages life to go on is by calling others around to join in blessing the Author of life. The more praise, the better; the more that join in, the better. Praise begets more praise—and more life. The psalmists seem to know the truth of the proverbial saying, "Laugh and the world laughs with you...." People naturally gather around someone who is positive, who conveys some sense of building a future. There is nothing that rallies most of us so much as a hopeful person.

Elements of the Psalms of Praise

Getting others to join in giving thanks gives shape to the psalms of praise. A call to others to worship always occurs in them—ordinarily at the outset, often in the middle or at the end, sometimes in all three spots. The *call to worship* is one of three units found in these psalms. It is often closely linked with the second unit, *naming the others* invited into prayer. Sometimes the congregation includes the ends of the earth, the sea, the world, all people, hills, rivers—in other words, a vast host of creation and humanity:

Let the rivers clap their hands
and the hills ring out their joy

at the presence of the Just Judge who comes,
who comes to rule the earth.
Yahweh will rule the world with justice
and the peoples with fairness. (Psalm 98:8-9)

The third unit is a spirited *account of God's actions*, the reason for
giving praise. This testimony from the psalmist serves to
motivate the hearers to give thanks also.

But we don't have to wait until we are called upon to feel
or express grateful prayer. We can enter into this attitude of
thankful wonder by reflecting on psalms already given to us. I
have always found Psalm 138 helpful for thanksgiving in
general. To begin, recall some favor God did or is doing for you
and/or your loved ones. If you are ready for some unbounded
praise, let the psalmist call you forth.

I thank you, Yahweh, with all my heart;
I sing praise to you before the angels.
I worship at your holy temple and praise your name,
because of your constant love and faithfulness,
because you have shown that you and your word are
    exalted.
You answered me when I called to you;
you built up strength within me.
All the rulers of the earth will praise you, Yahweh,
because they have heard your promises.
They will sing about your ways
and about your great glory.
Even though you are exalted, you care for the lowly.
The proud cannot hide from you.
Even when I am surrounded by troubles,
you keep me safe;
you oppose my angry enemies
and save me by your power.
You will do everything you have promised me;
Yahweh, your faithful love endures forever.
Complete the work that you have begun.
(Psalm 138:1-8)

Images of God in Praise Psalms

I find it easier to praise God out of experiences of well-being and wonder than out of my pain. It is much easier to feel grateful when I have just received a bonus rather than a rejection. In moments of belonging, reward and hopefulness, God appears more likable to me than in difficulties. When I am in a praising frame of mind, my mood matches that of the praise psalms.

Singing God's praises, however, is much more than satisfying a whimsical mood. Over a period of time, the psalmists associated some lasting images of God with their reasons for a gratitude which surpasses fleeting appreciation.

It is more characteristic to praise the Ruler of the universe when one understands one's place in it. We are very likely to give thanks to a strong and provident God when life is fulfilling; it's natural to speak to God as a Teacher and Counselor when there's evidence that Wisdom itself has encouraged life to flower. It is not surprising, therefore, that some images are more prevalent in the psalms of praise than in other psalms.

Look for these:

Creator and sustainer of life (Psalms 8, 65, 92, 95, 100, 104, 145-148)

Majestic ruler of universe (in fire, storm and cosmic glory) (Psalms 29, 93, 96-98, 150)

Royal ruler of all nations (includes messianic motifs) (Psalms 2, 20-21, 45, 72, 101, 110, 117)

Victorious leader and liberator (Psalms 47, 76, 114, 126, 149)

Teacher, guide, wise lawgiver (Psalms 19, 25, 34, 78, 111-112, 119)

Divine presence in the temple (Psalms 15, 24, 47, 84, 138)

Inner strength in the city (Psalms 46, 48, 122 and, perhaps, 87)

When praise erupts from the heart, the world takes on a new light. Developing a keener sense of wonder resembles being in love: The presence of the partner casts everything—

especially things once taken for granted—into a larger perspective. Psalm 93 takes a fresh look at the sea:

> The seas have lifted up, O Yahweh,
> the seas have lifted up their voice;
> the seas have lifted up their pounding waves.
> More powerful than the thunder of the great waters,
> mightier than the breakers of the sea—
> Yahweh is powerful on high.
> Your decrees stand firm;
> holiness adorns your house
> for endless days. (Psalm 93:3-5)

Exercise: Composing a Psalm of Praise

That text once awakened me to the sacredness of the ocean. The sea had already taken my breath away; then the psalmist inside me saw and sang the vastness of God over the waters of a vacation spot. Phenomenal good fortune led me there. I had survived two major surgeries in as many years; I had reason to rejoice. Feeling very full of life, I found the spray and sands to be the right material for my exultant praise, "A Psalm at Virginia Beach":

> Sing of the blessing of seagulls in flight
> Of boats on the horizon where a battleship lingers
> Sell what you have of pearls and sand dollars
> Of time and clockwise circumstances
> To belong for a while to the salty Sandbridges.
>
> Give glory, all you scurrying sand crabs,
> All you thin-legged gulls, soar on high.
> Give praise now, you barnacles clinging for life,
> And you mystified seaweed, lie in tongue-tangled
>   silence.
>
> We bend our knees before the waves,
> Asking in turn their homage as they bow before us.

45

Glory be for the threshold that constantly shifts
From division to encounter.

Divinity is here.
Also there.
Up and down.

Pouring itself out uncountable times—
As often as white caps arch around us
As often as we see forever in the sands,
As often as we do not hope for what is already washed
    away:

Children's castles,
An adult's momentary inspiration,
Young lovers' names etched on the beach,
Grandparents holding hands above their own footsteps.

Divinity is here
As often as we hope for the coming of the waves—
For cascades to come back never the same,
For the return to a favorite dune,
For the conch shell we might stumble upon,
For the tender spray we love replete with rough brine.
Glory be for all these wonders!

Try your hand at composing or paraphrasing your own
psalm of wonder and praise. A personal experience of
understanding, fulfillment or encouragement is a good starting
place. Let your memory guide you to some moment of elation,
excitement, contentment, extreme good luck, etc. Recall with
whom you first shared your good news: a spouse, a friend, a
neighbor. Or maybe you were surrounded only by the four
walls of your room when you shouted at discovering the extent
of your luck. Whoever or whatever was around then, whoever
you would now like to join you in thanking God, name
him/her/it/them in your call to worship.

Now that you have their attention, tell them what your
God—Creator, Savior or Spirit—has done for you. Let your
story tumble out of you with earthy and lively images to convey
the full force of your happiness. Feel free to dot your psalm
with your own images of God and with phrases of praise like,
"Thanks be to God" when your gratitude peaks.

5. When You Want to Wail

Psalms of Lament

The Jewish mourning custom, *shiva*, is a good way to lament a significant loss in your life. When a person close to you dies, you give yourself over to formal mourning for at least a full week. You don't go to work or cook or sweep the floor or do anything else. Other people take care of those things, allowing you to give yourself completely over to grieving. *Shiva* allows you to get into the depth of your experience, your gut, instead of denying or minimizing the enormity of your loss.

The pain of personal loss continues far beyond the first week, of course. Still, *shiva* lets you acknowledge your suffering by a period of wailing; it helps others understand and allows you to express your sadness. Neither their energy nor yours is tied up in pretense. Theirs is channeled into care and support; yours is directed toward dealing with the death. I would venture to say that even God is freed to move with you in your openness to divine consolation.

The concept of responding to death with a week of *shiva* can apply to other areas of life. Using a full seven days as a standard, you can attend other losses in due proportion. Suppose you wreck your car. How long do you need to grieve—one or two days? Or when you lose your billfold? Perhaps you can dedicate an afternoon to frustration not just because of the money—it's all those snapshots, the driver's license and the credit cards! What if someone only steals $20? Take 15 minutes to call and tell your trouble to a friend. Do yourself a favor: Whatever your loss, let your lament out in the presence of God and others whom you can trust.

Shiva provides a context for understanding the biblical songs of wailing. The name traditionally given to the wails is *psalms of lamentation* or, more simply, *laments*. If you're in the mood for mourning or are angry about how unfair life is to you or someone you care for, a full-blown lament is emotionally and spiritually healthful.

Psalms of lament are the Bible's complaint department. You can celebrate anger, remorse, fear and confusion in these wailing songs. You can give proper attention to the whole of your painful experience and your responses to it. Laments are sometimes called *psalms of supplication* because they are full of pleas for heavenly help to relieve suffering. They are *constructive* complaints which not only permit you to be yourself, but also allow God to be God in upsetting circumstances.

The laments bring three kinds of conditions to God's attention: loss (of life, health or friendship); suffering from sin; feeling lost.

Experiences of Loss

The mere prospect of losing life, reputation, health or an important relationship can be so unnerving that it stirs up bad dreams as we sleep. Conscious complaints and prayers burst forth when the danger draws closer. We may sense hostile forces afoot. Enemies of some sort threaten us—often through no fault of our own, which makes this experience different from loss through our own sinfulness.

One modern way that people today handle deepening anxiety is to attend a seminar on reducing stress. The psalmists' program for stress reduction is heard in throbbing wails. The psalms have found a way to see wrenching experiences from a larger perspective called "God." And from this perspective, all is not lost after all.

King David, psalmist par excellence, knew what it feels like to lose a friendship. He moans over betrayal by a supposed friend in the plaintive Psalm 55. Anyone who goes through divorce can understand the anguish of this psalm:

For it is not an enemy who reproaches me:
that I could bear.
It is not a rival who taunts me,
but you, my other self,
my companion and my close friend! (Psalm 55:12-13)

Rejection, insult and betrayal weigh him down. Bringing disappointment to prayer, David says, "But for me, I will call on God,/who will save me" (Psalm 55:16).

Perhaps another's neglect or ill will has affected you. Others are apparently taking advantage of the person who prays from a sickbed in Psalm 41. The patient cries aloud:

Those who come to see me are not sincere;
they gather all the bad news about me
and then go out and spread it everywhere....
They say, "You are fatally ill
and will never leave your bed again." (Psalm 41:6,8)

The author of Psalm 41 would understand the cynic who says, "When people ask you how you are, just tell them you're fine. Half of them don't really care—and the other 50 percent are glad you've got it!" Disillusionment accompanies the realization that a friend in need is a friend indeed—and a rare find, besides.

The laments turn to God for relief from whatever plight afflicts the psalmist. In Psalm 41 the patient groans,

Even my best friend—the one I trusted most,
the one who shared my food—
has turned against me.
Be merciful to me, Yahweh,
and restore my health. (Psalm 41:9-10)

Without specifying what will constitute that restoration, the sick person concludes with the reliance on Yahweh so typical of wailing songs:

I will know that you love me,
because they will not triumph over me.
You will help me, because I do what is right;

49

you will keep me in your presence forever.
Let us praise Yahweh,
praise the God of Israel now and forever!
Amen! Amen! (Psalm 41:11-13)

I once experienced a letdown from a friend. He stood up in public to lambaste a program I had coordinated and to criticize the speakers—whom he had recommended to me in the first place! Crushed and chagrined, I found grace was embodied in a woman who consoled me with a joke and several suitable remarks along with a hearty pat on the shoulder. Afterwards I was wary of the so-called friend and also glad for those who understood and saw the project through with me. In due time I wrote this "Psalm Lamenting a Tough Time":

Without warning or reason my balloon had burst,
Hot air spurted forth from every pore of my self!
My frustration mounted to tantrum peak
As I tried to hold on with strength I no longer had.
Why did this crisis arise? I complained to God:
How come my efforts are being jeopardized?
My energy is in crisis, I'm collapsing inside,
Struck by comments that pollute my optimism.

At the tip of my trauma, God came through
On the inside out of my very thin skin.
No sooner did I feel like deflated rubber
When a companion blew in like fresh air
With her sense of humor to help me bounce back:
The Spirit renewed what neither of us
Could drum up on our own steam.

Praise be to God whose creative ways
Burst forth through laughter that picks us up.
I rejoice that I trusted in the gentle wind
And the smile of perspective that is God's alone to give.
Thanks be to the One who remains Most High
By caring to love us when we are down.

Human Sin

Another cause for wailing is the suffering caused by sin—our own and that of the community with whom we associate. Numerous psalms have emerged from the human experience of being separated from God through one's own fault. Some of these prayers are labeled *penitential psalms*; they serve as acts of contrition. But they confess more than the penitent's offenses: They celebrate God's mercy with marvelous conviction.

Recall King David who committed adultery with Bathsheba, the wife of Uriah the general. The king's lust led him to arrange for her husband's death on the battlefield (see 2 Samuel 1). Acutely aware that he had abused Yahweh's trust and the integrity of the kingship, David lamented his offenses. Most of us try to keep a low profile in the wake of any public immorality; David went public with his scandalous behavior. Filled with keen shame and guilt, his sorrow knew no bounds. His wailing psalm begs aloud for forgiveness:

> In your goodness, O God, have mercy on me;
> with gentleness wipe away my faults.
> Cleanse me of guilt;
> free me from my sins.
> My faults are always before me;
> my sins haunt my mind.
> I have sinned against you and no other—
> knowing that my actions were wrong in your eyes.
> Your judgment is what I deserve;
> your sentence supremely fair. (Psalm 51:1-4)

The man groans with remorse as he roams through the palace halls in that psalm. All Israel could hear his lamentations about putting his relationship with God in jeopardy. If I had been one of his subjects, I would have wondered if the prayers for the king in other psalms (such as Psalms 20, 21, 101) had done any good at all.

David's rotten behavior required mighty repentance. Even then, only God's mercy could accomplish what David needed. Some evils are so gross that the sinner can be redeemed only by God's action. David seemed to know this; although he was sinful, he was not stupid. He did not compound his dilemma by covering over his immorality. He took responsibility, moved to make restitution, and threw himself on the mercy of the Savior:

> Out of the depths I cry to you, O God;
> God, hear my voice!
> Let your ears be attentive
> to my cry for mercy.
> If you, O God, mark our guilt,
> who can stand?
> But with you is forgiveness,
> and for this we revere you.
> I trust in you, God,
> my soul trusts in your word,
> My soul waits for you, O God,
> More than sentinels wait for the dawn,
> Let Israel wait for you.
> For with you is faithful love
> and plentiful redemption;
> God will redeem Israel
> from all their iniquities. (Psalm 130:1-8)

Notice that while David owns up to his wrongdoing, he accents God's merciful kindness. By pointing out Yahweh's compassion, perhaps David wants to nudge God into responding mercifully to one royal sinner! We can apply that outlook to our relationship with the Savior as well.

Feeling Lost

Feeling lost is a third disturbing experience worthy of wailing. A child screams in the middle of a grocery story because he can't find Mommy; he's lost. He does not know where to turn to soothe his loneliness and fright. A driver takes a wrong turn in a strange town; the longer it takes to get her bearings, the worse her panic grows. Think of the Jews wandering in the desert. How would it feel to be literally lost for 40 years? I would prefer finding my way out sooner, thank you.

Figuratively speaking, being lost may refer to times of psychological disorientation, times when things don't make sense at all. At such times we cry, "Why did this happen to me?" Everything we have lived by seems to be crumbling, and we feel confused and unsure in an absurd world. When everything seems upside down, we are like the child in the grocery store. We don't know where to turn for meaning, for God, for a sense of order. We wail for comfort:

> I cried aloud to you, O God,
> I cried, and you heard me.
> In the day of my distress I sought you, Yahweh,
> and by night I stretched out my hands in prayer.
> I lay sweating and nothing would cool me;
> I refused all comfort.
> When I remembered you, I groaned;
> as I pondered, darkness came over my spirit.
> My eyelids would not close;
> I was troubled and I could not speak.
> My thoughts went back to times long ago;
> I remembered years past.
> All night long I was in deep distress;
> as I lay thinking, my spirit was sunk in despair.
>
> (Psalm 77:1-6)

At the end of this prayer, the psalmist recalls the divine habit of giving guidance and begins to look trustingly for an encore:

> Your path led through the sea,
> your way was through mighty waters,
> and no one marked your footsteps.
> You guide your people like a flock of sheep,
> under the hand of Moses, Aaron, and Miriam.
>
> (Psalm 77:19-20)

Because God has redirected lost and exiled people before, relief is now in the psalmist's hopeful sight.

My own "Psalm of a Worrier" is based on the anxiety which many of us encounter during a sleepless night.

> God, tell me what's the matter with me?
> I cannot seem to wake up.
> Healer of all, what's the matter with you?
> Give me more reason to trust.
> My heart and mind are feverish with worry
> over things beyond my control;
> Like a violent virus and rampant as sin,
> it saps me of strength and soul.
> Every time I awake throughout the night
> I am anxiously sweating from troubles within.
>
> All night long my brain is a magnet
> attracting distressing thoughts,
> They center on me, only on me,
> not on your goodness, I'm sorry,
> But on my narrow nightmare of *oughts*:
> ought to do this, ought not to say that,
> ought to be appreciated,
> ought not to risk too much.
>
> Drive out my little dreads with your presence,
> God of my dreams,
> Turn me firmly toward
> life's fullness unthwarted.
> Help me live with a grateful spirit
> for the reality of my days.
> Then despite my worries and warts,
> I'll weary you with psalms of high praise.

That prayer recalls the humorous saying of Pogo, "We have met the enemy and they is us!"

Elements of the Psalms of Lament

Although these psalms display a range of reasons for lament, three elements recur:

The first characteristic is *shifting moods*. True to the tradition of oral prayer and to life itself, prayers of lament jump back and forth from doubt to faith. From decrying the enemy's ghastly misdeeds a psalm turns to look for Yahweh's help; from fear of persecution it shifts to reliance on God's intervention. This tension between describing one's troubles and anticipating divine deliverance appears in almost all the songs of wailing. When events shake our belief in God, then belief becomes the lived moment of faith. We might say, for instance, "I was on shaky ground and I knocked at God's door for help," or, "I felt helpless but I prayed intensely."

The next element is *disclosure*, the poetic description of the psalmist's dire straits. Not all the details are given, just enough to let readers and listeners know the extent of the trouble: "I became a whipping post, a nobody"; "People scoffed at me in my misfortune."

The third element is an *expression of confidence*. This ordinarily concludes the lament, although it can occur at any point (or points) in the psalm. The psalmist praises God's redemptive action: "When things were at their worst then Yahweh strengthened me," or, "It was when I hit bottom that my spirits began to rise, and for this I give thanks and praise to my Savior!" Even if vindication has not yet happened, the psalmist prays *as if* God has already acted—so strong is the reliance on Yahweh.

Psalm 102 illustrates these three elements in its first 12 verses. Because it laments misfortune pure and simple, its text can easily apply to a struggle with any enemy—oppressive people outside yourself or the dark forces within:

> Yahweh, hear my prayer
> let my cry for help reach you.
> Since I am in trouble,
> do not conceal your face from me.
> Turn and listen to me.
> When I call, respond to me quickly.
> For my days are vanishing like smoke,
> my bones burn like fire,
> my heart withers like scorched grass
> even my appetite is gone.
> And when I sigh,
> my skin clings to my bones.

I am like a pelican living in the wilderness,
or a screech owl haunting the ruins.
I lie awake moaning
like some lonely bird on the rooftop.
All day long my enemies insult me,
and those who used to respect me
use my name like a curse.
The bread I eat has become like ashes;
what I drink is mixed with my tears—
All because of your anger.
You lifted me up so you could throw me back down.
My days pass away like shadows;
I wither away like grass.
But you, Yahweh, endure forever;
Every age remembers you! (Psalm 102:1-12)

Images of God in Psalms of Lament

The laments expect God to be a good listener. The
wailings present Yahweh as genuinely concerned. Without
some flicker of that belief, the prayer could not get off the
ground. God is portrayed as one who can and will do
something to help the wailers through the struggle.

God's action is not always specified, for Yahweh is free to
choose to assist in any way; we cannot dictate. Rather than
remove the disease or destroy the enemy, God may decide to
strengthen the wailer to deal with the onslaught. Or God may
just remain *with* the sufferer no matter what the difficulty.
Frequently the lament ends on this last note: trusting in God's
promise to be by the psalmist's side. After praying as hard and
urgently as possible, the lamenter says, in effect, that the rest
is up to God.

The names the laments use for God indicate the nature of
the help one hopes for in the midst of severe trials. Below are
some images of God that have spoken to me out of the laments:

Merciful forgiver (Psalms 6, 32, 38, 51, 102, 130, 143)
Just judge (Psalms 11, 50, 52, 55, 58-59, 94)
Healer of human malaise (Psalms 39, 41, 43-44, 53, 77)
The one who answers our pleas (Psalms 31, 40, 71, 86)

A God who sends suffering (Psalms 44, 71, 73, 88, 102)
One who acts too slowly (Psalms 10, 13, 42, 83, 109)
The ultimate avenger (Psalms 3, 35, 64, 82, 140)

In all the laments, a trusting people in desperate circumstances cry out to God for whatever action, attitude or grace they need to proceed with dignity restored, sins forgiven and confidence renewed—ready for the next trial.

Exercise: Composing a Psalm of Lament

If you have ever felt woeful and begged God for help and strength, it might be beneficial to try your own hand at the psalm of lament. Read some of the psalms cited above. Consider how the three elements explained on pp. 54-55 fit your experience. Then let your song of wailing take shape in your heart. Do not limit your images of God to those presented above, but draw on whatever expresses your particular manner of addressing God and asking for help. You will learn the value of this kind of prayer by actually doing it.

The psalms of lament teach us that it is wholesome to look for God's help in hardship. "Let us pray," the psalmist invites. More precisely, "Let us summon the God who hears our laments to be the God who helps us in our losses." Surely that's not too much to ask of our God!

6. Singing of Well-Being
Psalms of Trust

Hardly anything lasts. When everything is on the upswing, we say, "It's too good to be true!" or, "All good things must come to an end." When things are going badly (from the trivial to the tragic), we take hope from the same reality: "Well, it can't last forever!"

In both good fortune and ill, it helps to look beyond the immediate for equilibrium. From the psalmists we receive a style of prayer which takes the present state of affairs seriously without depending merely on current conditions for lasting hope. They sing of God's steadfastness:

> O God of my salvation!
> Though my father and mother forsake me,
> you will still accept me....
>
> I believe that I shall see the goodness of Yahweh
> in the land of the living!
> Wait for Yahweh;
> be strong, and let your heart take courage.
> Yes, wait for God! (Psalm 27:9b-10, 13-14

As songs of well-being, the psalms of trust represent a mainstay of biblical spirituality. They witness to the tenacious presence of Yahweh through the best of times and the worst of times. They exude confidence, the single most enduring mood in the psalter. Where does this conviction come from? One story can tell the tale.

A Story of Faithful Love

Put yourself in the shoes of the Jewish widow Naomi, whose Gentile daughters-in-law Orpah and Ruth have just lost their husbands, Naomi's only offspring. As the Book of Ruth opens, the funerals are over and the three widows stand at a crossroads in their relationship with one another.

The two younger women are natives of Moab, where Noami's family sought refuge from hunger years before. Their beliefs and customs had been unfamiliar to their Hebrew husbands. After all their work to build understanding between their people, the women's lives have turned upside down. Though the cause of death goes unreported in the book, its shattering effects are evident in the trio's conversation about where and how to pick up their lives.

Naomi will return to her hometown and undoubtedly will have to make big adjustments. She recognizes her bitterness that fate's cruel blow has dashed her expectations of grandchildren. With neither mate nor progeny to care for her, Naomi faces want, perhaps even condemnation. Maybe some folks in the town will resent her sons' "interfaith marriages." "Had she done anything to avoid this taboo? Then perhaps she deserves her forsaken state."

Although Naomi is bereft of a ready-made place right now, her people will not reject her outright. Her difficulty will lie in providing for herself day to day and in playing social roles all seen as minuses: a former wife, a has-been mother-in-law, a childless mother. Feelings of belonging and acceptance in her community could prove problematic for her.

Proudly overcoming her dejection, Naomi tells Orpah and Ruth to go home with her blessing. They deserve the chance for a fresh start without obligations to her. She refuses to entrap them by playing on their guilt or pity. They owe her nothing.

Orpah responds by accepting Naomi's gracious words. Tearfully the first daughter-in-law departs.

Ruth decides to follow her heart's lead and stay with noble Naomi. Ruth puts their relationship on a new footing by her surprise plans. If Naomi can make unilateral announcements, so can Ruth! Naomi can hardly believe her ears when Ruth states that she intends to join her mother-in-law in her return home.

Naomi cannot talk Ruth out of her determination to go to Judah. Naomi hopes she's not taking on a tiger by agreeing to the companionship of this headstrong young woman. It's a sweet risk Naomi will have to take; Ruth seems to love the old woman beyond former legal ties. What loyalty and tenderness she shows in her firm promise: "Wherever you go, Naomi, I'll go too: wherever you live and die, I will too. Your people and mine are the same from now on. They always will be, to my dying day" (see Ruth 1:16-17).

Stunned, Naomi cries with joy over this turn of events. Ironically, her son Mahlon has given her a daughter after his death! Noami has reason to wonder if Ruth has learned something about the God of the covenant. Or are the Jews about to learn something new about God's fidelity?

Ruth embodies more than random luck. She stands out as the astounding one who consciously pledges personal care to Naomi. Naomi intuits the hand and presence of the living God in the person of Ruth, and that is the way the story has been understood for a long time.

We are Naomi. Ruth signifies the undeserved kindness and compassion of God in our regard. A God who is so steadfast communicates more than a momentary stroke of fine fortune. Yahweh's intense commitment endures no matter what. Surely this God is worthy of our confidence and prayers of trust.

'Daily' Prayer

Praying with firm trust is a hallmark of psalmody in general. An extra dose of confidence characterizes some psalms more than others, however. These songs of trust express the spiritual energy that sustains us over the long haul as well as on any given day. I distinguish these calmer psalms from those that deal with the marked highs and lows of our situations. These psalms give a feel for relying on the Creator, Savior and ultimate Source of Life—*every day*, not just at time of high drama.

Whoever first sang Psalm 139, for instance, was aware of God's sustenance from the womb:

> You created my inmost being
> and knit me together in my mother's womb.
> For all these mysteries—
> for the wonder of myself,
> for the wonder of your works—
> I thank you.
> You know me through and through
> from having watched my bones take shape
> when I was being formed in secret,
> woven together in the womb. (Psalm 139:13-15)

The singer takes immense comfort from the divine knowledge, understanding and guidance.

The psalm reminds me of Patricia, who makes it a yearly practice to celebrate confidence. Each birthday she meditates on developments over the past year: relationships, spiritual progress and major decisions. Her review compares her situation with that of the preceding birthday. By this method she becomes conscious of how God, with her active cooperation, has readied her for another year of life.

The amazing thing about Patricia's annual reflection is her ability to see connections instead of conflicts between her personal growth and the giftedness of her life. Her annual review engenders not only gratitude, but also trust in Goodness with a capital G. Within and beyond the goodness of her own growth, she discovers a God who gives her reason for continuing to trust life. The exercise is all the more remarkable since Patricia suffered life-threatening illnesses as a young adult. She is happy to have made it to middle age, which she welcomes as a time of opportunity.

Like my friend Patricia and the singer of Psalms 27 and 139, you and I can gain confidence through the human process of maturing. Confidence is born of having lived long enough through better and worse, sickness and health to affirm the words of William Allen White: "I am not afraid of tomorrow for I have seen yesterday and I love today."

Elements of the Psalms of Trust

Like the laments and hymns of praise, the songs of trust display their own special qualities: (1) A sense of well-being; (2) interplay of emotions; and (3) emphasis on God's dependability.

First and foremost is the *sense of well-being*. It is built on the bedrock assurance that God has seen you through thick and thin and, like Ruth, refuses to be parted from you by death or danger. The same theme appears in St. Paul's Letter to the Romans; the apostle proclaims that nothing can separate us from the love of Jesus Christ (see 8:31-39).

Next, although the trust theme is definitely dominant, the psalmist may frequently bring in *other emotions*, such as contempt for those who victimize others:

> Their plan is only to destroy.
> They take pleasure in lies.
> With their mouths they utter blessing,
> but in their hearts they curse. (Psalm 62:4)

A more pleasant emotional addition is gladness over an uncluttered life-style:

> Yahweh, my heart has no false pride;
> my eyes do not look too high.
> I am not concerned with great affairs
> or things far above me. (Psalm 131:1)

The free association of minor themes occurs in part because the psalms are primarily oral prayers (see pp. 28-30). These free associations make the songs true to life. Other sentiments also accompany the stories about memorable incidents which gave rise to trust in the first place. Recalling how one survived can stir up intense feelings about the struggle itself.

On the other hand, psalms of confidence concentrate on *divine dependability* to guarantee that survival. No matter what the circumstances (and the psalmist always fills you in on the main elements), the prayer repeats the theme of trust:

> For God alone my soul waits.
> My help comes from God,
> who alone is my rock, my stronghold, my fortress:
> I stand firm. (Psalm 62:1-2)

The same wording is repeated in Psalm 62:5-6. The psalmist drives the point home with indisputable evidence that the unwavering support of Yahweh has meant the difference between life and death.

Psalms of trust are probably an outgrowth of earlier pleas prayed during great hardship. Now that things are under control, enemies overcome, bad times in the past, the psalmists review how the prayer was answered. They reflect on who pulled them through and once again conclude that God has been holding them up on eagles' wings all along. Their prayer distills their appreciation and confirms the heavenly guardian:

> I lift my eyes to the mountains.
> Where is help to come from?
> My help comes from Yahweh,
> who made heaven and earth.
> Yahweh does not let our footsteps slip!
> Our guard does not sleep!
> The guardian of Israel
> does not slumber or sleep.
> Yahweh guards you, shades you.
> With Yahweh at your right hand
> the sun cannot harm you by day,
> nor the moon at night.
> Yahweh guards you from harm,
> protects your lives,
> Yahweh watches over your coming and going,
> now and for always. (Psalm 121:1-8)

These three building blocks of the psalms of trust are almost predictable, considering the nature of Yahweh. The language and structure correspond to an understanding of God as faithful and merciful. Reasons for confidence in God are sketched: God's efforts which favored or rescued those in need (the psalmist, community or nation). Repeated expressions of trust and well-being speak the psalmist's appreciation of graces received and usually spill over into outright thanksgiving.

Images of God in Psalms of Well-Being

You may have noticed the combination of strong and gentle images of God in the psalms of trust. The maternal aspect of Yahweh appears along with the ability to give secure protection. This God feels with us and inspires our confidence with divine action on our behalf. The table below offers a summary of such images:

> Nurturing parent (Psalms 71, 121, 131 or, by contrast, 27)
> Tender redeemer or rescuer (Psalms 11, 70, 91, 124, 141, 144)
> Shepherd (Psalms 23, 80)
> Protector and shelter (Psalms 4, 61-62, 68, 125)

Confidence is not quickly restored when we have a setback. In the wake of tragedy and blatant unfairness, the battle against bitterness can be monumental; getting stuck in what went wrong can be a strong temptation. The effort to believe again, to trust again, is complex. These clear and direct images of a caring God serve both to bolster us and to calm us for the next trial, which we know is bound to happen.

For most of us life is jagged ups and downs. We do well to travel like Naomi, with the knowledge that, wherever we go, God will come with us. The psalmist hopes in a God who has managed to hang in there—not to do everything for us, but to help us out and help us along our way. This model of faithfulness occurs over and over in the psalms:

> What if Yahweh had not been on our side?
> Answer, Israel!
> "If Yahweh had not been on our side
> when our enemies attacked us,
> then they would have swallowed us alive,
> in their furious anger against us.
> Then the flood would have carried us away;

the water would have engulfed us—
the raging torrent would have swept over us."
Let us praise Yahweh,
who has not let our enemies destroy us.
We have escaped like a bird from the hunter's trap;
the trap has been broken, and we are free!
Our help comes from Yahweh,
the Maker of heaven and earth. (Psalm 124:1-8)

Exercise: Composing a Psalm of Trust

Since trust takes a longer time aborning than lamentations and
hymns of praise, it might take longer to compose a psalm of
trust than either of the other two. You may find it easier to let
your prayer grow out of a psalm that is already composed. For
instance, Psalm 131 pictures God as a mother holding us in her
arms. A hug from anyone tends to reassure us, but from God
it's infinitely comforting.

To prepare to pray Psalm 131, bring to mind some worry
you have—anxiety over how you're doing in some big area of
your life, concern about your life-style or goals. Whatever
worries you, try to become attentive to it. Keep it with you
throughout the prayer as you let yourself be hugged:

Yahweh, my heart has no false pride;
my eyes do not look too high.
I am not concerned with great affairs
or things far above me.
It is enough for me to keep my soul still and quiet
like a child in its mother's arms,
as content as a child that has been weaned.
Israel, hope in Yahweh,
now and for always! (Psalm 131:1-3)

Searching my own temptations to lose confidence
sometimes, I am bolstered to continue my prayer in response
to that psalm:

66

God of the hopeful, I know what I'm doing when I say you're timelessly trustworthy. In all my yesterdays you have been there for me. Usually you have created opportunities for me through the goodness of other people. However you have done it, you have been with me, leading forward to this day. I am counting on you to accompany me into the tomorrows of my life. Jesus heroically confirmed the durability of your Word—for yesterday, today and forever. Now I know what he meant. With his Spirit I pray like the wise psalmist: Sustain me as you have promised, that I may live; disappoint me not in my hope. Glory be to the Creator and to the Savior and to their Holy Spirit; as it was in the beginning, is now and will be forever. Amen.

Psalm 139:1-19 is another fine choice to spark your own prayer (omitting the fiery verses near the end). To prepare for praying through it, think back over your life and the favors you received from parents or parental figures. Relish all there is to relish in your remembering. Then say Psalm 139 aloud, slowly, and let it connect with your memories. Do not force any verse to tie in. A few of them may not fit at all. Notice that this prayer is addressed to a God who is committed to being with you even when you might be tempted to escape into oblivion or to go it alone. All the more reason to trust.

If, on the other hand, you are at a stage in your life when you would like to write your own prayer of confidence, simply locate an event or period in your experience when you felt God undeniably came through for you. Then try to incorporate the three main features of the trust psalms (see pp. 63-66) in a paragraph or poem.

A Last Word

I cannot leave the psalms of trust behind without tipping my hat to David. His undauntable spirit of trust pervades every psalm in the book. I offer a poem honoring David as the patron of those who want to drink the rich wine of the psalms. The entire psalter is devoted to God; I give this one small toast to David, "The Psalmic Ballad for David: Shepherd, Sinner, King":

David, you were a courageously crazy kid,
Killing Goliath but loving Jonathan as you did.
Do you know the extent of your love, shepherd boy?
Pray tell me, O David, O David.

Thank God Bathsheba did not have to die
To cover the truth of your sin and your lie.
She suffered the loss of your son, yes.
What standards, O monarch, can you apply?
. Bless God for the free love and forgiveness.

Yahweh has blessed you with royal oil,
You've been forgiven for sin and spoil,
Do you know the depth of your passionate praise?
Sing it, King David, O sing it, O.
Trust God with your song, sing it, O.

7. Beyond the Psalms

Sex, Politics and Religion in Prayer

Though the psalms come from a very distinct Hebrew culture, the universality of their concerns has helped to keep them vital in many times and cultures. Certain universal archetypes, which eminent psychologist Carl G. Jung said exist in the collective subconsciousness of the human race, also appear in the psalms: images of father and mother, sexual energies as represented by husband and wife, figures of authority like kings and queens, the tension between the Creator and the void of no-God.

We can see these archetypes in our own culture today. For instance, contemporary American society claims to have no place for kings and queens. Some even say royalty is an outmoded concept. Yet we line the streets and keep long vigils to catch a glimpse of visiting royalty. Even citizens who claim they are "not morning people" will get up before dawn to see live television coverage of an English royal wedding. And many others will tune in to reruns or pore over newspaper coverage.

Psalm 45, a nuptial song, manifests this same fascination with pageantry. Beginning with a dedication, the psalmist poetically sets the stage for a royal wedding. Then the princely bridegroom enters, wonderfully robed and sensuously perfumed with myrrh, aloes and cassia—exotic equivalents of after-shave and talc. He is summoned to come forth to receive the assembly's accolades and prayers. The psalm extols his heroism, his elegance, his ability to protect his people and his moral virtues—a desirable young man indeed!

In the context of prayer, the psalm lauds the groom's handsomeness and the bride's physical beauty as if seeing each through the other's eyes. As the bride's procession begins, you can virtually hear the trumpet accompanying this dazzling queen from her chambers to his. Finally, the prayer wishes them fertility and long-lasting honor—all in good taste:

> My heart overflows with a goodly theme;
> I address my verses to the king;
> my tongue is like the pen of a ready scribe.
> You are the fairest of all,
> grace is poured upon your lips;
> therefore God has blessed you forever.
> Gird your sword upon your side, O mighty one,
> clothe yourself with glory and majesty!
> In your splendor ride forth victoriously
> for the cause of justice and to defend the truth;
> let your right hand show your wondrous deeds!
> Your arrows are sharp
> and pierce the hearts of your enemies.
> Your divine throne endures forever and ever.
> Your royal scepter is a scepter of equity;
> You love justice and hate wickedness,
> Therefore God, your God, has anointed you
>   with the oil of gladness;
> your robes are all fragrant with myrrh and aloes and
>   cassia.
> From ivory palaces stringed instruments bring you joy;
> daughters of kings come to meet you;
> at your right hands stands the queen in gold of Ophir.
> Hear, O daughter, consider, and turn your ear;
> forget your people and your ancestor's home.
> The king will desire your beauty.
> The people of Tyre are here with gifts,
> the richest of the people seeking your favor.
> The princess is decked in her chamber
> with gold-woven robes;
> in many-colored robes she enters with her virgin
>   companions,
> her escort in her train.

With joy and gladness they are led along
as they enter the palace of the king.
The place of your ancestors your children shall have;
you will make them rulers through all the earth.
I will cause your name to be celebrated in all
    generations;
therefore the peoples will praise you forever and ever.

(Psalm 45:1-17)

Sex and Prayer

Psalm 45 is the only biblical psalm with an explicitly sexual
theme. But sexuality appears in other biblical contexts (as well
as in other sacred texts and non-biblical psalms). After all,
union between man and woman is a recurring human event
that transcends geographical and historical boundaries.

A very developed description of two lovers occupies the
Song of Songs. The account is graphic enough that St.
Benedict's Rule, which recommends daily Scripture reading,
cautions against the use of this particular book of the Bible at
night by monks of weak understanding. The enduring appeal
of mutual love is celebrated in the Song, whose style resembles
Psalm 45, but whose content and details are more lavish and
intimate.

Sexual imagery emerges in other biblical canticles as well
as in additional ancient texts which, for one or another reason,
never became part of the official Judeo-Christian Scriptures. An
example of God acting as a lover toward Israel appears in the
prophet Hosea, whose wife's infidelity mirrors the people's
unfaithfulness to Yahweh. The prophet's tender pursuit of his
wife parallels God's relentless passion for the Chosen People.
Is Hosea (or God) a glutton for punishment, or is it a case of
knowing that the powerful experience of love-making
strenthens the marriage tie?

The latter motif surely underlies the wedding song
Yahweh sings to celebrate and renew the bonds of the covenant
in the canticle in Zephaniah 3:14-18. We also hear it in the lyrical
passages of Isaiah 54:5-8. In Isaiah 62:1-5 the image is explicit:
Divine love seeks Jerusalem as a bride.

Other ancient texts rely on feminine sexual imagery.

71

While these texts are part of the Jewish and Christian heritage, they have never became part of the "canon" of the Bible—the official list of books in our Judeo-Christian Scriptures. Two collections, both dating from the period between the writing of the Old Testament and the writing of the New, were discovered in the first half of the 20th century. The *Odes of Solomon* represent a school of Jewish mysticism; the 25 psalms found in the Dead Sea scrolls come from the Essenes, an ascetic community contemporary with Jesus.

Bearing some likeness to the canonical psalms of the Bible, these extra-canonical odes and hymns support our understanding of a compassionate, tender God. Because of their explicit female imagery, they also reinforce for women a sense of the sacredness of their own sexuality. These images are quite compatible with those of Psalm 45, the Song of Songs, and the prophets Hosea, Zephaniah and Isaiah. They help to balance the biblical bias toward masculine images of God.

One song from the *Odes of Solomon*, for example, refers to God's breasts:

> A cup of milk I was offered
> and I drank its sweetness as the delight of the Lord.
>
> The Son is the cup
> and he who was milked is the Father
> and he who milked him is the Holy Ghost.
>
> His breasts were full
> and his milk should not drip out wastefully.
>
> The Holy Ghost opened the Father's raiment
> and mingled the milk from the Father's two breasts
>
> and gave that mingling to the world, which was
>   unknowing.
> Those who drink it are near his right hand. (Ode 19)

The *Odes* were not excluded from our Scriptures because of their sexual images but because overall their theology tends to downplay the value of the body and the need for total involvement—body, mind and heart—in the mystery of salvation.

Some recently discovered Hebrew psalms are ancestors of the present biblical psalter. These beautiful poems often contain phrases and verses which also appear in the biblical canon. The non-biblical Psalm 11 presents the *maternal* aspects of God:

> You have chosen me father to the sons of kindness,
> nurse to men of wonder,
> and they have opened their mouths like babies sucking
>   at the breast,
> like a tender child playing in its nurse's bosom.
> You raised my horn above those who revile me,
> who attack
> but shake like windy trees.
> My enemies are chaff in the winds,
> and my domination is over the children of error.
>
> You healed my soul
> and raised my horn,
> and I will glow in seven folds of light
> with beams from your glory.
> You are everlasting light
> and help me to walk to you.

Poetic literature like the Hebrew hymns, the *Odes of Solomon*, and the biblical canticles enrich psalmic prayer in at least one other way: They use the language of mysticism. For centuries Christian mystics have drawn on sexual metaphors to convey the rapturous closeness in experiences of God. Maybe their intensity accounts in part for their appeal.

Politics and Prayer

Another cross-cultural theme found in the psalms is respect for law and a sense of history.

In ancient Israel authority was divinely given by Yahweh—first to the early judges and later to the king. It was up to the king to demonstrate God's consummate care for widows and orphans, the weak and the poor. The ruler was to reflect God's will and God's ways to all the people. That is why David's lust and murder (2 Samuel 11) and his grandson Rehoboam,'s excessive taxes (2 Chronicles 10) flagrantly violated the office. Psalm 68:5-7 presents the ideal which the sovereigns should follow:

> "Father of the fatherless, mother of the orphan,
> and protector of the weak is God.
> God gives the desolate a home in which to dwell
> and leads out the prisoners to freedom...."

While the political assumptions of our American republic are different from those of Israel's theocracy, the psalms can help us pray for God's assistance in caring for those in our charge as well as in working for the rights and well-being of the less fortunate.

> Alleluia!
> Praise Yahweh, O my soul!
> I will praise, you, Yahweh, all my life;
> I will sing praise to you as long as I live.
> Put not your trust in rulers,
> in humans in whom there is no salvation.
> When their spirits depart they return to the earth;
> on that very day their plans perish.
> Happy those whose help is the God of Jacob and Rachel,
> whose hope is in Yahweh, their God,
> The maker of heaven and earth,
> the sea, and all that is in them;
> Who keeps faith forever,
> secures justice for the oppressed,
> and gives food to the hungry.
> Yahweh, you set captives free
> and give sight to the blind.
> You raise up those that were bowed down
> and love the just.
> You protect strangers;
> the orphan and the widow you sustain,
> but the way of the wicked you thwart.
> Yahweh shall reign forever;
> your God, O Zion, through all generations. Alleluia.
>
> (Psalm 146:1-10)

The dentist who does charity work for the destitute helps carry out this prayer. The doctor who removes the cataracts of an elderly patient frees the dependent patient from relying on government through personal outreach. Our government's role is to facilitate our efforts to be agents of more abundant life.

I know one retired sister whose ministry is letter-writing. Her letters to prisoners in dire straits invite the convicted people to explore and express struggles of a spiritual nature, especially reconciliation. She encourages their sense of dignity with her own respect. She has helped to "set captives free." Sometimes she takes personal involvement a step higher by advocating a prisoner's cause, again via the written word.

The doctor, the dentist, the sister all make themselves available to help God carry out the requests voiced in Psalm 146. Actions like these keep our prayer honest. We dare not take God's name in vain by praying empty petitions that we have no intention of helping God fulfill. On the other hand, when we pray the psalms with the intention of standing behind our pleas, we become aware of our own potential to create possibilities for others.

Having a sound political sense means knowing how to organize and use social power to accomplish your goals. The politics of the psalmist include enlisting Yahweh's power through prayer while letting God mobilize us in the service of the good. The goal of the infinite Creator is continually to transform inhuman and less-than-human situations into something better. Ancient Hebrew and modern American traditions share that dual task of praying and working for the improvement of the globe. The motto "In God we trust" arises from both cultures. Trust needs its ally, determination, to move forward "with liberty and justice for all."

True Religion and the Psalms

Another way contemporary Americans can resonate with ancient psalmists is in their respect for law. Despite the high crime rate in many of our cites, we Americans by and large make and keep laws that promote good social order. Most of us observe traffic ordinances and pay taxes according to the rules and are disturbed by violations of law. If we did not take legislation seriously, we would not bother trying to influence elected representatives to change inadequate laws.

What does this have to with psalmody? How can it help us relate to those biblical prayers? Concern for law, according to the psalmist, is the way of wisdom. The psalms that deal with the social and domestic order are the *wisdom* psalms. Often they are called *didactic* ("teaching") psalms because they teach us how to make our way in the world. They point out ways that lead to life and ways that lead to death.

The psalter opens with this realistic contrast: "For God knows the way of the just,/ but the way of the ungodly ends in ruin" (Psalm 1:6). One view holds that the whole Book of Psalms falls into the category of wisdom literature. In support of this opinion, the first psalm tells us that what we need is a resolve to pursue the way of wisdom. The rest of the psalms tell us over and over what has and hasn't worked. Finally, Psalm 150 closes with praise for what God has done to help us find life in abundance. The total picture is a panorama of what the good life is all about.

Biblical wisdom centers around Yahweh's commands. God lays down cosmic laws for creation (Psalms 104 and 148). Human beings receive special commands from the God of the covenant through Moses. Psalm 81 refers to these Ten Commandments, calling people to be faithful to Yahweh for their own good. The psalmist sings in worried tones, thinking that the reason the nation is oppressed by enemies is failure to live by Yahweh's wisdom:

> Listen, my people, while I admonish you.
> Listen to me, O Israel:
> You shall have no strange god among you
> nor bow down to any foreign god.
> I am Yahweh, your God,
> who brought you up from Egypt.
> But my people did not listen to my voice,
> and Israel would not obey me;
> so I sent them off, stubborn as they were,
> to follow their own way.
> If only my people would listen to me,
> if Israel would only walk in my ways,

I would soon humble their enemies
and lay a heavy hand upon their persecutors.

(Psalm 81:9-15)

I wonder if the Chosen People grew impatient when they
found out that life requires more than simply obeying the rules.
Obedience and cooperation do not necessarily get us where we
want to go. You know the saying, "Nice guys always finish
last." The wisdom psalms insist the opposite is true, that
goodness will win reward. Tobit, whose story is also part of the
wisdom literature, is the kind of model the psalms praise.

Tobit: A Wisdom Story

The Book of Tobit opens with testimony to its main
character's upright life. Living in exile in Babylon, Tobit was as
generous as could be to his family and his people. While some
of his people sacrificed to the false gods of their foreign
oppressors and flattered their masters to protect their own
skins, Tobit doggedly kept the values and beliefs he had grown
up with.

One evening Tobit and his wife Anna were ready to
celebrate a festival with their son Tobiah. Tobit sent his son to
invite a less-fortunate relative to the feast. But the young man
burst back into the house with the horrible news: A kinsman
had been strangled downtown! Worse yet, the murderers had
callously pitched the corpse into the street where it was still
lying like a heap of trash. Because Jewish funeral customs had
been forbidden by the pagan king, no one dared to touch the
body.

Tobit immediately proceeded to break the royal decree
and give the dead man a proper burial before sundown. His
neighbors jeered: "How stupid! What good will this do for the
fellow now? Why risk your fool neck to do this futile deed in
the open among strangers who can't understand? It won't bring
anyone back to life and may attract the ire of our rulers." But
Tobit didn't let others' jeering deter him from doing what he
thought was right.

After the burial, Tobit bathed and lay down out in the
courtyard to relax. Surely he had earned a good night's sleep

and a sweet dream. Instead, a bird flew over his head and dropped dung straight into Tobit's face! The mess hit his eyes, causing blindness. That freakish accident cost Tobit four years of medical treatments and major adjustments in the household. A cousin helped cover the mounting costs for a couple of years, but then moved away. Tobit finally had to depend on his wife's skill with a loom to make ends meet.

Then Tobit remembered that he had deposited a large sum of money with a distant kinsman. He had not returned for it because the roads in that direction had become too perilous to travel. But now the situation was so desperate that Tobit sent his son Tobiah to reclaim the money.

As Tobiah set out, his father's advice to fear God and live rightly ringing in his ears, he met Raphael, an angel in disguise. With the angel's help, Tobiah returned home not only with the money, but also with a new bride and a magical cure for his father's blindness.

Finally Tobit's faith in Yahweh paid off. His sight was restored. The younger couple took care of Tobit and Anna in their old age, which was filled with constant praise of God for all that had been done for them. They overcame the results of the accident and the four (it felt like 20) years of struggle without any obvious assistance from the divine Healer. But it didn't matter any more. All was redeemed.

Whatever doubts they might have had during their ordeal, Tobit and Anna never ceased living the way of wisdom. They are immortalized in the Bible for their endurance in the ungodly city of Nineveh. Their son and his wife lived to see the fall of Nineveh. Tobit and Anna could not have asked for a better reward for their piety.

I can imagine that during their lives, Anna, Tobit and Tobiah achieved moral virtue by taking instruction from the wisdom psalms. This series of psalms would have served Tobit and his family well at key points in their lives. The sequence below roughly parallels Tobit's story:

> Psalm 112: fairness and generosity
> Psalms 25, 119: inspiration; God's view
> Psalm 54: faith during persecution
> Psalm 116: devotion to the true God

Psalm 86: courage to face an ordeal
Psalm 70: trust despite the odds
Psalm 102: long-suffering resignation
Psalm 29: readiness for a breakthrough
Psalm 71: steadfastness over the years
Psalm 144: fortitude
Psalm 126: sense of renewal, restoration
Psalm 16: hope in life beyond the grave

Can't you imagine Tobit leading his household in this prayer?

Alleluia!
Happy those who fear Yahweh
and joyfully keep God's commandments!
Children of such as these will be powers on earth;
each generation of the upright will be blessed.
There will be riches and wealth for their families,
and their righteousness stands firm forever.
Even in the darkness, light dawns for the upright,
for the merciful, compassionate, and righteous.
These good of heart lend graciously,
handling their affairs honestly.
Kept safe by virtue, they are always steadfast
and leave an everlasting memory behind them.
With a trusting heart and confidence in Yahweh,
they need never fear evil news.
Steadfast in heart they overcome their fears;
in the end they will triumph over their enemies.
Quick to be generous, they give to the poor;
their righteousness stands firm forever.
People such as these will always be honored.
This fills the wicked with fury
until, grinding their teeth, they waste away,
vanishing like their vain hopes. (Psalm 112:1-10)

Alas, the happy ending does not always materialize as it did in the Book of Tobit. In the Gospels we read of a man named Jesus who dealt lovingly with men and women alike, who gave to Caesar and to God according to their dues, and whose human lifetime ended in suffering and severe ignominy. In his honor, I offer this poem, "My Childhood Speaks to

Christ," in the spirit of the wisdom psalms:

Who's who is not a game you play
when you are suppering your last of days.
Pinning the tail on a donkey or an apostle
is no way to treat a traitor.
Red Rover comes over with sticks and clubs
and changes to Judas overnight.
No time left for Mary's son to ask, "Mother, may I?"
but only "Father,
I will
thy will
by golly."
When your skin is jumpier than your feet
hopscotch is as accurate as any other
numbers game and the throwing of stones
then dice at the foot of unbroken bones.
When heavy heavy hangs over thy head
what else can be chanced to redeem it
except to become It, tagged a Savior?
Breaking all the rules of the game
and taking your turn at letting them break you,
you count to 2,000 years or more only
to find there is no place left to play hide
and seek the living among the dead.

A Last Word

Sex, politics and religion: a trinity of human realities surpassing cultural confines. We may avoid such controversial subjects except with trusted friends, but there is no reason to exclude these universal experiences from prayer. On the contrary, there is good reason to bring our problems and pleasures into our conversations with the God of love, power and wisdom. It all makes for a wholesome explosion of prayer in the real world. From this "Big Bang" many more possibilities could evolve.

Appendix A: More Exercises

1) Relating the Psalms to the Gospels

When we pray the psalms, we imitate Jesus, who grew up nourished by Jewish prayer and who was undoubtedly influenced by a spirituality based on the psalms. The Gospels frequently portray him and his contemporaries quoting the psalms directly or referring to some aspect of them. Find in your Bible the following passages from the Gospels and the related psalms:

Gospels	Psalms
Matthew 27:46; Mark 15:34	22:2
Luke 1:49	111:9
Luke 1:52	113:7; 75:7-8
Luke 1:53-54	107:9
Luke 1:54-55	98:3
Luke 1:68	106:48
Luke 1:72	111:9
Luke 23:46	31:6
John 12:13	118:26

Read Matthew 27:46. Then read through all of Psalm 22. Try to pray Psalm 22 from different viewpoints: Jesus on the cross, your own suffering, someone else's suffering.

Another way to meditate on the same Gospel passages is to try praying the associated psalm from the viewpoint of someone else in the Gospel scene (a principal character or an observer in the crowd). Using the same texts over and over but from different viewpoints can lead to new insights.

2) Addressing the God of Many Faces

Many images of God enrich the psalter. From the list below, select an image that attracts you. Praise or petition God by this name for something in your life right now. Try writing your prayer. You might begin like this: "The psalmist and I praise [ask] you, God [name the image], because..." Let your prayer flow from that point on. Pray boldly as psalmists do.

Angel or winged spirit (Psalm 17:8; 18:11; 63:8)
Archer (Psalm 7:13-14)
Barbecuer (hot coals) (Psalm 120:4)
Bather (Psalm 108:9)
Builder (Psalm 8:4)
Covenant-maker (Psalm 89)
Father (Psalm 2; 89:27-28)
Farmer (Psalm 65:10-14)
Grower (Psalm 80:9-10, 16)
Handsome man (bridegroom) (Psalm 45:3)
Has hands like us (Psalm 63:9)
Hater (Psalm 11:5)
Lifesaver (Psalm 40:3; 144:7)
Light (Psalm 27:1)
Lover (Psalm 45)
Master of day and night (Psalm 74:16)
Mother (Psalm 139:14)
Reader of human hearts (Psalm 138:6; 139:1)
Refuge of the oppressed (Psalm 9:10)
Rock (Psalm 28:1)
Shield (Psalm 3:4; 18:31)
Sleeper (Psalm 44:24)
Undresser (Psalm 108:9)

There are many other images of God in the psalms. If you keep a personal or spiritual journal, jot down the images that speak to you as you read or pray the psalms. Record the prayers you write over a period of a month. At the end of the month, take 20 minutes to review your psalm prayers. What do the images you use tell you about where your relationship with God seems to be going? Where you would like to be growing?

3) Rearranging a Psalm

Choose any psalm verse which has spoken to your heart (for example, Psalm 119:105, "A lamp to my feet is your word, a light to my path"). Copy the words on a blank sheet of paper or a page in your journal. Then play with the physical arrangement of the text. Rewrite the verse, capitalizing the words that jump out at you and putting all the rest in lower case. Rewrite again, placing capital letters in the middle of important words. Arrange and rearrange the words on the page. Slant a line of the text upwards or downwards diagonally as you please. If you associate certain feeling tones with particular colors, rewrite the verse with magic markers. Enhance the text with calligraphy or line drawing, if you can. Write your heart out with whatever instrument you use— pencil, pen, marker or even computer—according to the meaning you feel within the text.

This kind of movement with a psalm text can be fruitfully shared in a prayer group. Let different members explain what led them to shift a psalm verse this way or that. Visualizing and verbalizing what moved someone to see meaning in a psalm from a certain angle offers insights.

Whether you are alone or with others, pray the rearranged verse aloud after your reflection. Words may take on new significance after this active type of meditation.

Continue quiet group sharing by creating "Psalm Stations." Post the psalm graphics in a place where group members can move from "station" to "station" at their own pace.

4) Praying Day by Day

Using psalms for your daily private prayer can help form you in their spirituality. One way to do this is to start your day with psalms for the morning. Use only a portion of a psalm if that is all that speaks to you on a given day. Some selected psalm verses for morning are Psalm 5:3-4; Psalm 108:3-5; Psalm 19:6-7; Psalm 110:3b.

The same approach can be used for evening prayer. Try Psalm 3:5-6; Psalm 121:1-3; Psalm 4:4-9; Psalm 131:1-3; Psalm 63:5-9; Psalm 134:1-3.

Punctuate the rest of your day with psalmic ejaculations so that psalmody becomes part of you. Use phrases that have struck you while dwelling on a psalm (see Chapter Three) or in the exercises above. If you have written the text down, post it on your desk, windowsill or wherever you will see it throughout the day. Here are some verses that are short enough to make good ejaculations:

Heed my call for help.... (Psalm 5:2a)

...Praise the God of Israel now and forever!
(Psalm 41:13b)

...May the whole earth be filled with God's glory!
(Psalm 72:19b)

O God, do not be silent.... (Psalm 83:1a)

...God's love is strong....(Psalm 117:2a)

Let everything that breathes praise Yahweh.
(Psalm 150:6)

5) Praying the Liturgy of the Hours

Formerly called the Divine Office, the Liturgy of the Hours is the public, communal prayer of the Church. The Liturgy of the Hours grew out of Jewish prayer times and modes. Its four basic elements (hymns, psalms, readings and prayers) require the psalms as the core content and attentiveness to time as its atmosphere. For further study and prayer alone or with others, suggested titles follow:

Benedictine Sisters of Erie, Inc., *Five-Week Psalter* (Benet, 1985). Distribution of psalms, antiphons and responses in Morning, Evening and Vigil services for those already familiar with the Hours; inclusive language. Musical settings of Magnificat and Benedictus canticles in complementary booklet, *In Praise of the God of All* (Benet, 1985).

Morning and Evening Prayer (Liturgical Press, 1978). Prayerbook for personal use; distributes psalms for morning and evening prayer according to accepted usage; easy to follow on one's own.

Morning Praise and Evensong: A Liturgy of the Hours in Musical Setting (Fides Publishers, Inc., 1973). Simple chants and hymns with cantor and congregation parts marked to enable easy use in parishes.

The Liturgy of the Hours, Study Text VII (United States Catholic Conference, 1981). A fine introduction by the Bishops' Committee on the Liturgy for individual or group study on concept, development and practice of Liturgy of the Hours; discussion guides, glossary and quoted references from selected Church documents.

Roguet, A.M., *The Liturgy of the Hours* (E.J. Dwyer Publishing Co., Australia, 1971). Explanation and commentary on each part of the Hours in light of the Vatican's *General Instruction* (1971 edition) with translation included for ready reference.

Taft, Robert, *Liturgy of the Hours in East and West* (Liturgical Press, 1985). Historical treatment; traces differences and connections between Roman and Eastern rites.

Appendix B: Psalm Versions

Many versions of the psalms are available to today's pray-er. Biblical scholarship has produced new translations of the entire Bible. In addition, popular interest has led to numerous translations and paraphrases of the psalms themselves. Finally, the psalms as songs continue to inspire musicians and composers. Below you will find a list of resources for all these forms with brief notes regarding their appeal or limitations.

Bible Translations

Anchor Bible, Psalms I-III. For scholars and lay alike who wish faithful translations and informative notes.

Good News Bible. Contemporary English; inexpensively bound; standard language.

New American Bible. Modern English with background footnotes and cross-references.

New English Bible. Retains use of intimate address to God (*thee, thou*); sparse notes; ecumenically acceptable.

The Jerusalem Bible. Information and cross-references in introduction and footnotes; addresses God as Yahweh.

The Living Bible. Refreshing contemporary style, language.

Psalm Translations

Berrigan, Daniel, *Uncommon Prayer: A Book of Psalms* (Seabury, 1978). Abundant imagery and unusual grammatical structures; useful for private meditation or oral reading by a single voice.

Botz, Paschal, *Runways to God: The Psalms as Prayer* (Liturgical Press, 1979). Entire psalter accompanied by commentary on Christian spirituality and scholarly background; suitable for personal knowledge and prayer.

Brandt, Leslie, *Psalms Now* (Concordia, 1973). Highly popular paraphrases which reinterpret texts for contemporary Christians; style appropriate for informal use; may offend classicists or purists; good for youth.

Hanson, Richard, *The Psalms in Modern Speech*, three volumes (Fortress, 1968). Standard usage and arrangement of text in sense lines; clear, faithful translation; useful for private or group prayer.

International Committee on English in the Liturgy, *The Liturgical Psalter* (ICEL, 1974, 1975, 1977). International standard English usage and verse/stanza arrangements; liturgical use intended, approved.

Jewish Publication Society of America, *The Book of Psalms* (JPSA, 1972). Loyal to traditional Hebrew text in direct, clear way; very adaptable to liturgical use in Liturgy of Hours or with Jewish-Christian dialogue/prayer groups.

Leach, Maureen, and Schreck, Nancy, *Psalms Anew* (St. Mary's Press, 1986). Non-sexist language referring to God and humanity; canticles of Zachary and Mary included; tables of psalms for use in four-week cycle of Liturgy of the Hours.

Oosterhuis, Huub, *Fifty Psalms* (Herder & Herder/Continuum Books/Seabury, 1969). Selected psalmody in inspirational, personalized mode; suitable for prayer in common.

Rosenberg, David, *Blues of the Sky* (Ultramarine, 1987). Interpretations of original Hebrew Book of Psalms in striking contemporary metaphors; single voice or meditation preferable to choral recitation because of minimal capitalization and punctuation.

Shepherd, Massey H., Jr., *A Liturgical Psalter for the Christian Year* (Liturgical Press, 1976). Ecumenical collection of 59 psalms in sense stanzas with appendices applying to the rest of the Bible and Church year. (See also Shepherd's *Psalms in Christian Worship* [Augsburg, 1976] with complementary background.)

Sullivan, Francis Patrick, *Lyric Psalms: Half a Psalter* (Pastoral Press, 1983). Contemporary recasting of selected psalms in beautiful lyrics; interspersed sketches supply meditative visuals in this large-type volume.

Taylor, Charles L., *Layman's Guide to 70 Psalms* (Abingdon, 1973). Selected psalms for devotion and study by Episcopalian author of earlier volume, *Let the Psalms Speak*; brief statements on Hebrew origins, Christian perspectives; author's own psalm prayer after each commentary.

Van Zeller, Hubert, *The Psalms in Other Words* (Templegate, 1964). Readable versions approaching paraphrases in classical mode; suitable for private or group use; some adaptable as orations.

Selected Musical Settings

The Grail Gelineau Psalter, Unison Singer's Edition (G.I.A. Publications, Inc., 1968). Includes 18 canticles.

Haugen, Marty, *Psalms for the Church Year* (G.I.A., 1984). A collection for pastoral liturgists.

Psalms, A New Translation, Singing Version, by Joseph Gelineau (Paulist, 1953). Easily applicable to group prayer.

Songs For a New Creation (Augsburg, 1982). In the tradition of Lutheran hymnody.

Winston, Colleen, "Psalm Songs" in three-part set, *The Word In Sight and Sound* (Ikonographics, 1977). Instructive audiocassette and meditative filmstrip present fresh versions of Psalms 23, 145 and 148; includes printed music that can be used in prayer services or classroom.

Worship II (G.I.A. Publications, 1975). Includes musical settings for psalms in hymnody section. Consult index for psalms used in other ways, e.g., eucharistic and sacramental celebrations.